CLASSROOM
READING
INVENTORY

SEVENTH EDITION

CLASSROOM
READING
INVENTORY

NICHOLAS J. SILVAROLI

Arizona State University

Madison, Wisconsin • Dubuque, Iowa • Indianapolis, Indiana
Melbourne, Australia • Oxford, England

Book Team

Executive Editor *Stan Stoga*
Editor *Paul L. Tavenner*
Production Editor *Diane Clemens*
Visuals/Design Developmental Consultant *Marilyn A. Phelps*
Visuals/Design Freelance Specialist *Mary L. Christianson*
Publishing Services Specialist *Sherry Padden*
Marketing Manager *Pamela S. Cooper*
Advertising Manager *Jodi Rymer*

Brown &
Benchmark

A Division of Wm. C. Brown Communications, Inc.

Executive Vice President/General Manager *Thomas E. Doran*
Vice President/Editor in Chief *Edgar J. Laube*
Vice President/Sales and Marketing *Eric Ziegler*
Director of Production *Vickie Putman Caughron*
Director of Custom and Electronic Publishing *Chris Rogers*

Wm. C. Brown Communications, Inc.

President and Chief Executive Officer *G. Franklin Lewis*
Corporate Senior Vice President and Chief Financial Officer *Robert Chesterman*
Corporate Senior Vice President and President of Manufacturing *Roger Meyer*

Illustrations by Craig McFarland Brown

Cover and part opener designs by Jeanne Regan

A Times Mirror Company

Library of Congress Catalog Card Number: 92–54759

ISBN 0–697–12586–6

Permission to reproduce the Inventory Records is given freely to those who adopt this text for classroom use.

Printed in the United States of America by Wm. C. Brown Communications, Inc., 2460 Kerper Boulevard, Dubuque, IA 52001

10 9 8 7 6 5 4 3 2 1

CONTENTS

PREFACE

The Classroom Reading Inventory (CRI) is designed for teachers and prospective teachers who have not had prior experience with informal reading inventories.

To become better acquainted with my version of an informal reading inventory, teachers and prospective teachers should:

1. Read the entire manual carefully.
2. Study the specific instructions thoroughly.
3. Administer the CRI to at least two students.
4. Keep in mind that successful individual diagnostic reading procedures are developed gradually through experience. Techniques, procedures, and ideas must be adapted to each testing situation.

I believe teachers and prospective teachers will begin to gain confidence with the CRI after administering this informal inventory seven times.

As a final note, let me express my gratitude to my wife, Jann Silvaroli. I would also like to express my indebtedness to my friends, Warren Wheelock and Lyndon Searfoss, for their invaluable contributions to the development of the CRI.

We wish to thank the following reviewers for their insightful comments: Lane Gauthier, University of Houston, Diane Allen, University of North Texas, and Lora Friedman, Christopher Newport University.

Nicholas J. Silvaroli

INTRODUCTION

Purpose of the Classroom Reading Inventory

Norm-referenced tests (group reading tests) are used to determine student reading achievement. This group testing approach might be called classification testing. The results classify students according to a global reading achievement level, which is frequently interpreted as a student's instructional reading level. The Classroom Reading Inventory (CRI), a version of an informal reading inventory, is an individual testing procedure that attempts to identify a student's reading skills and/or abilities.

Differences between Individual and Group Testing

The difference between individual and group testing can be illustrated by a bried description of the reading performances of two fifth-grade students, Joan and Don. Their norm-referenced test (NRT) results are:

Joan (10 years 11 months old): NRT 4.2 overall reading
Don (11 years 2 months old): NRT 4.2 overall reading

When we examine their NRT results, these two fifth-grade students appear to be about the same in age and overall reading achievement. However, data obtained from their individual CRIs indicates that there are significant *instructional* differences between these two students.

On the Graded Word Lists of Part 1, Joan pronounced correctly all the words at all the grade levels, one through six inclusive. It is evident, therefore, that Joan is well able to "sound out" or "decode" words. However, when Joan read the Graded Paragraphs of Part 2, she was unable to answer questions about these paragraphs even at a primer-reader-level of difficulty.

Don, on the other hand, was well able to answer questions about these same paragraphs up to a second-grade-reader-level of difficulty. However, his phonetic and structural analysis, or decoding, skills were inadequate for his level of development.

The results obtained from NTRs concerning reading achievement tend to *classify* students as average, above average, or below average in terms of their reading achievement. As teachers, however, we need much more specific information if we are to be able to develop meaningful *independent* and *instructional* reading programs for every student. The CRI is designed to provide teachers with just such specific, and necessary, information.

GENERAL INFORMATION

What Is the Classroom Reading Inventory (CRI)?

The CRI is a diagnostic tool for teachers to be used at either the elementary, junior high or middle school, and high school or adult levels.

At the elementary level, this seventh edition departs significantly from previous editions of the CRI. All previous editions followed what might be called a SUBSKILLS format, which diagnosed the student's ability to decode words (word recognition) and answer questions (comprehension). This logically followed the type of instructional reading programs used, and still being used in most elementary school classrooms. Therefore, the CRI continues to use the SUB-SKILL FORMAT in Form A.

In recent times reading programs have been shifting to a different instructional format. This period of change in reading instruction brings with it a wide variety of terms and concepts. For example, terms such as *whole language, literature-based,* or *literacy programs* appear to carry their own concepts and interpretations. The CRI uses the term LITERATURE FORMAT for these newer instructional reading programs. This seventh edition departs from previous editions by using *one* SUBSKILL FORMAT, Form A, and introducing *one new* LITERATURE FORMAT in Form B.

What follows is a brief overview of the four forms used in this seventh edition of the CRI:

Form A—elementary level traditional SUBSKILLS format
Form B—elementary level LITERATURE format
Form C—junior high or middle school level SUBSKILLS format
Form D—high school or adult level SUBSKILLS format

Form A retains its traditional SUBSKILLS format. This is the same format used in all previous CRIs. The graded words (Part I) and the graded paragraphs (Part II) were changed. The graded words will continue to be used for phonetic analysis and to estimate where to begin the graded paragraphs. The Inventory Record for Teachers remains as it has in all previous CRIs. Form A has changed most of the words (Part I) and story selections (Part II). (See pp. 7–12 for specific instructions on administering Form A.)

Form B introduces some of the current concepts used in a LITERATURE approach to basic reading instruction. The oral reading selections in Form B *will not* be followed by traditional questions; rather, the student will be asked to make predictions and retell (discuss) the selections with the teacher. The procedures, teacher/student interactions, and Inventory Record are different from all previous editions of the CRI (see pp. 13–20 for specific instructions on administering Form B).

Forms C and D use the traditional SUBSKILLS format presented in Form A. The graded words and paragraphs are identical to those used in the sixth edition. Therefore, this edition does not change Forms C and D in any way.

What Are the Major Uses for Each Form?

Form A (pp. 39–70) elementary level traditional SUBSKILLS format is designed to assess the students application of:

word recognition skills
comprehension skills
spelling ability
listening capacity

Form B (pp. 71–88) elementary level LITERATURE format is designed to:

provide information about student's comprehension ability
quickly identify the student's ability to read comfortably at some level of difficulty

Form C (pp. 89–117) is designed for junior high or middle school students. The administration, marking, and scoring procedures are similar to those procedures used for Form A. However, the story content in Part II is appropriate for students in this age group. Form C differs from the two forms at the elementary level in that:

the story content for all eight grade levels deals with mature topics
preprimer (PP) and primer (P) levels are not included in the graded word lists or paragraphs
pictures or illustrations are not included in Form C
spelling and listening are not included

Form D (pp. 119–147) is designed for high school students and adults. The administration, marking, and scoring procedures are similar to Forms A and C. Form D is also similar to Form C in that Form D uses mature content. Preprimer and primer levels, pictures, spelling, and listening are not included in Form D.

Can These Four Forms be Interchanged?

Forms A and B have different purposes and *should not* be interchanged at the elementary level. Forms A and B use less mature content and should not be used with older students (Form C) or adults (Form D). However, Forms C and D can be interchanged for older students.

How Does Form B Differ from Form A?

Form B (Literature Based) differs from Form A (SubSkill) as follows: Form B evaluates various aspects of the student's comprehension ability. Form A evaluates the student's ability to decode and answer different types of questions. Allow me to be more specific. The procedure, in Form B, asks the student (1) to use the picture and title to **predict** what the selection might be about, and (2) **retell** the aspects of the selection; i.e., characters, problems and outcome. Form A evaluates the student's ability to answer fact (F), vocabulary (V), and inference (I) questions.

Both forms use a **quantitative** scale for the evaluation of individual reading ability. However, Form B assigns a number to the **quality** of the student responses. Again, allow me to be more specific. When the student is discussing characters in the selection, he or she is given zero credit for no response and 5 if the teacher judges the response as outstanding. In Form A, if the student answers 4 of the 5 questions, he or she is judged to be "independent," in comprehension, at that level.

Both forms provide evaluative data. However, Form B is designed to assess the student's ability to use a retelling procedure (to indicate student's ability to comprehend) and to find the student's comfortable reading level. Form A is concerned with decoding words and the number of questions answered correctly (to indicate student's ability to comprehend).

Are There Other Differences?

One other main difference has to do with the active or passive role of the teacher. When using Form A the teacher tends to be more passive. Form A requires the teacher to record correct or incorrect responses and to use these responses to determine subskill needs, in the areas of word recognition and comprehension. Form B requires the teacher to take a more active role. For example, the teacher needs to encourage the student to make predictions about the selection and to determine the student's knowledge of the selection through discussion. In addition, the teacher must be willing to make **qualitative** judgments about student responses.

Are There Ways in which These Forms Are Similiar?

Both forms provide the teacher with realistic instructional information. Both forms attempt to establish beginning instructional reading levels. For example, if a fifth grader is reading comfortably on a third-grade reading level, both forms can provide teachers with this instructional information.

As previously stated, Forms C and D have **not** been altered.

Is the CRI Used with Groups or Individuals?

All four forms are to be used with individual students. The Spelling Survey, included in Form A, may be used with the total class (see Specific Instructions p. 12 for an explanation of how parts of the CRI are to be administered).

What Is Background Knowledge Assessment?

A student's background knowledge plays a crucial part in the reading comprehension process. As Taylor, Harris, and Pearson (1988) have stated: "People comprehend reading material by relating the new information in the text to their background knowledge."[1] It follows, then, that the teacher should make a quick assessment of the student's background knowledge before the student is asked to read any Graded Paragraphs.

Administration Time and Cost Appear to Be Important. WHY?

Busy teachers do not have a great deal of time to test individual students. Therefore, each form of the CRI is designed to be administered in *twelve minutes or less*. However, more than twelve minutes, per administration, is likely to be needed when learning to give the CRI. Cost is kept to a minimum by allowing teachers to reproduce the Inventory Records for each form.

What Readability Formula Was Used in the Development of the CRI?

The Fry Readability Formula[2] was used for Forms A, C, and D. The reading selections for Form B are based on the SEER,[3] a technique for estimating readability level, developed by Singer (1975).

1. Taylor, B., Harris, L., and Pearson, P. D. *Reading Difficulties*, Random House, NY, 1988, p. 226.

2. Fry, Edward B. *Reading Instruction for Classroom and Clinic*. McGraw-Hill Book Company, NY, 1972, 230–234.

3. Singer, Harry. The SEER Technique: A Non-Computational Procedure for Quickly Estimating Readability Level, *Journal of Reading Behavior*, 1975, *VII*, 3.

Helpful Hints for Forms A, C, and D

Some helpful hints based on questions teachers have asked over the past 20 years are:

1. When administering the Classroom Reading Inventory, a right-handed teacher seems to have better control of the testing situation by placing the student to the left, thus avoiding the problem of having the inventory record forms between them.
2. When administering Part 2 (Graded Paragraphs), the teacher should move the student booklet before asking the questions on the comprehension check. Thus, the student is encouraged to utilize recall ability rather than merely locate answers in the material just read.
3. The word count, given in parentheses at the top of each paragraph in the inventory record for teachers, that is, Form A, Part 2–Level 3 (96 words), does not include the title of the paragraph "Strange Facts about Elephants."
4. Students living in different parts of the United States react differently to the Graded Paragraphs. If you or your students react negatively to one or more of the paragraphs, feel free to interchange the paragraphs contained in Form C and Form D.
5. It is important to establish rapport with the student being tested. Avoid using words such as "test" or "test taking." Instead use "working with words" or "saying words for me."
6. Before the teacher can analyze the types of word recognition errors a student can make, he or she will need a basic understanding of the word recognition concepts listed on the Inventory Record Summary sheet; such as, blends, digraphs, short vowels. (See p. 30 for a reference regarding basic word recognition concepts.)
7. When a student hesitates or cannot pronounce a word in Part 2 (Graded Paragraphs), the teacher should *quickly* pronounce that word to maintain the flow of the oral reading.
8. Testing on the Graded Paragraphs of Form A, Part 2, should be discontinued when the student reaches the Frustration Level in *either* word recognition or comprehension.
9. Pictures have been eliminated from Forms C and D because it is believed that the Background Knowledge Assessment, used at the beginning of each oral paragraph, is all that is necessary to establish background for the story to be read.
10. The scoring guide on Form A, Part 2, of the inventory record for teachers causes some interpretation problems. For example, the guide for Form A, Part 2—Primer "Our Bus Ride" is as follows.

SIG WR Errors		COMP Errors	
IND (Independent)	0	IND (Independent)	0–1
INST (Instructional)	2	INST (Instructional)	1½–2
FRUST (Frustration)	4+	FRUST (Frustration)	2½+

Should IND or INST be circled if a student makes three or four significant word recognition errors? It is the author's opinion that (a) if the student's comprehension is at the independent level, select the independent level for word recognition; (b) if in doubt, select the lowest level. This practice is referred to as *undercutting*. If the teacher undercuts or underestimates the student's instructional level, the chances of success at the initial point of instruction increase.

S P E C I F I C   I N S T R U C T I O N S

For Administering Form A
(To Be Used in the Elementary Grades 1 to 6)

Part 1 Graded Word Lists *Form A*

Purpose To identify specific word recognition errors and to estimate the approximate starting level at which the student begins reading the Graded Paragraphs in Part 2.

Procedure Present the Graded Word Lists, starting at the preprimer (PP) level and say:

"Pronounce each word. If you are not sure or do not know the word, then say what you think it is."

Discontinue at the level at which the student mispronounces or indicates he or she does not know five of the twenty words in a particular grade level (75 percent). Each correct response is worth five points.

As the student pronounces the words at each level, the teacher should record all word responses on the inventory record for teachers.[4] Corrected errors are counted as acceptable responses in Part 1. These recorded word responses may be analyzed later to determine specific word recognition needs.

Sample _____

1	came	$\underline{+}$		
2	day	$\underline{+}$		
3	up	$\underline{DK}$	(don't know)	(error)
4	was	$\underline{saw}$		(error)

Part 2 Graded Paragraphs *Form A*

Purposes:
1. To estimate the student's independent and instructional reading levels. If necessary, estimate the student's frustration and listening capacity levels (see p. 8 for levels).
2. To identify significant word recognition errors made during oral reading and to estimate the extent to which the student actually comprehends what he or she reads.

---

4. The Inventory Record for Teachers is a separate record form printed on standard 8 1/2-by-11 inch paper. Note: teachers have the publisher's permission to reproduce all, or any part, of the inventory record for teachers, Form A pp. 59–70, Form B pp. 81–88, Form C pp. 107–117, and Form D pp. 137–147.

Procedure Present the Graded Paragraphs, starting at the highest level at which the student recognized all twenty words in the word list, Part 1. Ask the student to read the story "out loud." Tell the student that you will ask several questions when he or she has finished.

What follows is a brief explanation of each of the four *levels* that apply to Forms A, C, and D. These four levels are usually abbreviated and referred to as Independent (IND), Instructional (INST), Frustration (FRUST), and Listening Capacity (LC).

Levels

Independent Level

The teacher's first aim is to find the level at which the student reads comfortably.[5] The teacher will use the independent level estimate in selecting supplementary reading material and the library and trade books students will read on their own. Since this is the type of reading students will be doing for personal recreation and information, it is important that the students be given reading material from which they can extract content without hazards of unfamiliar words and concepts.

Instructional Level

As the selections become more difficult, the student will reach a level at which he or she can read with at least 95 percent accuracy in word recognition and with 75 percent comprehension or better. At this level the student needs the teacher's help. This is the student's instructional level,[6] useful in determining the level of textbook that can be read with teacher guidance.

Note: Most classroom teachers tend to be most interested in the student's Independent (IND) and Instructional (INST) level. However, the Frustration (FRUST) and Listening Capacity (LC) levels are included in the event the teacher feels the need to obtain such data.

Frustration Level

When the student reads a selection that is beyond recommended instructional level, the teacher may observe symptoms of frustration such as tension, excessive finger-pointing, slow halting word-by-word reading, and so on. Comprehension will be extremely poor; usually most of the concepts and questions are inaccurately discussed by the student. This represents a level that should be avoided when textbooks and supplementary reading material are being selected.

Listening Capacity Level

The teacher is asked to read orally more difficult selections to determine whether the student can understand and discuss what was heard at levels beyond the instructional level, it is assumed that the reading skills might be improved through further instruction, at least to the listening capacity level. Listening Capacity can be useful for classroom teachers who do not have students with "special needs."

5,6. The actual number of significant word recognition and comprehension errors permissible at each graded level can be found in the separate inventory record for teachers.

Recording Word Recognition Errors

In 1982, Pikulski and Shanahan[7] reviewed research on informal reading inventories. One of their conclusions was: "errors should be analyzed both qualitatively and quantitatively."

In previous editions of the CRI, it was assumed that all word recognition errors were weighted equally. As such, the teacher was asked merely to **quantify** word recognition errors. This edition requires the teacher to deal not only with just counting errors (quantitative) but to think about what the student is actually doing as he or she makes the error (qualitative).

In general, a word recognition error should be judged as *significant* (high weighted) if the error impacts or interferes with the student's fluency or thought process. *Insignificant* (low weighted) word recognition errors are minor alterations and do not interfere with student fluency or cognition; for example, student substitutes *a* for *the* before a noun, or, infrequently omits or adds a word ending.

The following is designed to enable teachers to make qualitative judgments and examples of significant (high weighted) and insignificant (low weighted) word recognition errors. It is impossible, however, to account for all possibilities. Therefore, teachers are advised to use this information as a guide to establish their own criteria for developing a qualitative mindset by which to determine whether the word recognition errors are significant or insignificant.

Significant and Insignificant Word Recognition Errors

The CRI recognizes the following five common word recognition error types.

1. The student does not recognize word and *needs teacher assistance*. This is symbolized by placing a *P* (for pronounced) over the word not recognized. This is always regarded as a significant error.

    P
    Example: The turkey is a silly bird.

2. The student *omits* a word or part of a word. This is symbolized by drawing a circle around the omitted word or word part. Infrequent omissions are considered insignificant word recognition errors. Frequent omissions are significant.

    Example: The cat chased the bird(s) Or, it was a (very) hot day.

3. The student *substitutes* a word for the word as given. This is symbolized by drawing a faint line through the given word and then writing the word substituted above it. This type of error is judged to be significant if it impacts or interferes with fluency or cognition. However, it may also be judged as insignificant if it does not interfere with fluency or cognition.

    grin
    Example: *Significant:* Baby birds like to eat seeds and ~~grain~~.

    a   *woods*
    Insignificant: He went to ~~the~~ store. Or, the children were lost in the ~~forest.~~

7. Pikulski, John, and Shanahan, Timothy. "Informal Reading Inventories: A Critical Analysis" in *Approaches to Informal Evaluation of Reading.* John J. Pikulski and Timothy Shanahan, eds. Newark, Delaware: International Reading Association, 1982.

4. The student *inserts* a word into the body of a sentence. This is symbolized by the use of a carat (∧) with the inserted word above the carat. Insertions are usually regarded as insignificant word recognition errors because they tend to embellish what the student is reading. However, if the insertion changes the meaning of what is being read it should be judged as significant.

Example: *Insignificant:* The trees look ∧*so* small.

Significant: The trees ∧*don't* look small.

5. The student *repeats* a word(s). This is symbolized by drawing an arc over the repeated word(s). Repetitions are usually considered to be insignificant errors because it is believed that the student is repeating an "easy" word(s) to gain time in decoding a more "difficult" word. However, excessive repetitions suggest the need for more reading practice, and they should be judged as significant.

Example: *Insignificant:* The crowd at the rodeo stood up.

Significant: They were bound for the salt springs near the . . .

As teachers become accustomed to thinking (qualitative) about why students make the errors they do, they will become more attuned to qualitative analysis of word recognition errors. As such, they will begin to better understand the decoding process and what mediates error behavior. Here are some examples of enhanced awareness on the part of teachers regarding qualitative analysis.

Example: The bird(s) *is* ~~are~~ singing.

Here we have an error of omission and an error of substitution. The first error, *omitted s* caused the second error, substituting *is* for *are*. If the student did not substitute *is* for *are* language dissonance would occur.

Example: How high ~~we are~~ *are we*.

Here we have two word substitution errors or a reversal of word order. These errors were caused by the first word *How*. How, at the beginning of a sentence, usually signals to the reader that it will be a question. This is just what the reader did; anticipated a question and made it into a question.

Example: ~~It is~~ *It's* a work car.

Here two words are contracted due mainly to the fact that it is more natural to say *it's* than *it is*.

Remember, it's not a case of how many errors (quantitative) but, rather, what caused the errors (qualitative). The more you become accustomed to thinking about error behavior, the better you will be able to understand the decoding process.

Marking Comprehension Responses (Part 2)

After each graded paragraph the student is asked to answer five questions. The separate Inventory Record for teachers labels questions as follows:

(F) Factual or Literal
(I) Inference
(V) Vocabulary

Suggested answers are listed after each question. However, these answers are to be read as guides or probable answers. The teacher must judge the adequacy of each response made by the student.

Partial credit is allowed for all student answers to questions. In most cases it is helpful to record student responses if they differ from the listed suggested responses.

Scoring Guide

What follows is the actual scoring guide used for level 5 (fifth grade), Form A page 67.

Scoring Guide WR Errors (SIG)		COMP Errors	
IND	2	IND	0–1
INST	6	INST	1½–2
FRUST	11	FRUST	2½+

Note that the scoring guide for this level, as well as all other levels in Part 2, uses error limits for the students; IND (independent), INST (instruction), and FRUST (frustration) reading levels.[8]

Thus, the guide suggests that when a student reads the selection entitled, "Electric Cars" (Form A, Level Five) and makes two SIG (significant) WR errors, the student is able to IND (independently) decode typical fifth grade words. Six SIG errors at this level suggests an INST (instructional) level. Eleven SIG errors suggests that the student is (FRUST) frustrated, in WR, at this level. The same scoring procedure should be applied to the comprehension portion of the guide.

One final factor in the use of this guide: In order for the teacher to determine realistic independent and instructional levels, the student responses to words and questions must be evaluated. The scoring guide provides estimated levels; however, the teacher needs to make the final diagnosis.

Summary of Specific Instructions

Step 1   Rapport. Make the student comfortable. Complete the top of the INVENTORY RECORD (Name, grade, age, date, teacher, and administered by) for the Form to be used. (See p. 6 for Helpful Hints.)

Step 2   Part 1 Graded Word Lists

Step 3   Part 2 Graded Paragraphs

---

8. See page 8 for a discussion of these levels.

Step 4 Begin Part 2, Graded Paragraphs at the highest level in which the student knew all 20 words in Part 1

Step 5 Background Knowledge Assessment (p. 5)
Before each graded paragraph, engage in a brief discussion about the story to be read. Attempt to get the student to reveal what he or she knows about the topic, and try to get the student to make predictions about the story. If the student has some background knowledge, rate student as adequate. If little or no background knowledge is apparent, mark inadequate. If using either Form C or D, exchange stories hoping to obtain a more appropriate selection.

Step 6 Graded Paragraphs. Ask the student to read the selection orally. Be sure the student understands that he or she will be asked to answer questions after each paragraph in Form A.

Step 7 Ask questions and record student responses if they differ from suggested responses.

Step 8 If the student experiences FRUST (frustration) in either Part 1 (WR) or Part 2 (COMP) stop at that point.

Step 9 Complete Inventory Record, use information from Part 1 and Part 2 to determine estimated levels.

Spelling Survey

Purpose: To obtain additional data on the student's ability to integrate and express letter-form, letter-sound relationships.

Procedure: Select a group of children who have completed Part 1 and Part 2. Begin at Level 1 (representative first-grade words). Level 2 is composed of representative second-grade words.
Discontinue at the level at which five of the ten words are missed. It is recommended that the teacher administer only one or two levels at a given sitting. The results should be scored and analyzed after each administration. Students who have reached the cut-off point should return to their desks and study quietly. See pages 149–151 for Graded Spelling Survey words.

S P E C I F I C   I N S T R U C T I O N S

For Administering Form B
(To Be Used in the Elementary Grades 1 to 6)

Introduction

Before dealing with the specific purposes and procedures used in Form B, it is necessary to provide information about two ways a student can demonstrate comprehension. These are the abilities to (1) **make predictions** and (2) **retell** the story in the student's own words.

The ability to retell a story (after reading) is believed to reflect comprehension by allowing the student to translate the story into the student's own words or reconstruct text information.

Form B (literature-based) divides the two abilities into four scorable parts (see p. 15 for a discussion of what the author means by scorable parts).

Student Ability	Scorable Parts
Predicting	1. *Predicting*—the use of pictures and title to anticipate story or selection content.
Retelling	2. *Character(s)*—the use of characters to deal with essential elements. *Problems*—those elements used by the characters, in the story, to identify problems or reach goals. *Outcome*—usually deals with how the characters solved the problems or attained the goals.

*Traditionally, reading instruction has required students to read and then answer questions as a way of developing and assessing comprehension. It seems reasonable to assume that the ability to make predictions and retell the story are usually not taught outside of most literature-based programs. If this is true, and students are in a traditional program, the author suggests that the teacher must decide to use Form A (traditional) or teach students how to predict and retell **before** administering Form B (literature).*

Preparing Students for Individual Evaluation

In the elementary school (grades 1–6) reading evaluation tends to occur near the beginning of the school year. Therefore, it is recommended that **before administering Form B,** the teacher needs to **model** the predicting and retelling procedure with the whole class or small groups, teaching these procedures.

What follows is a discussion of how to prepare students to make predictions and retell stories in their own words. This will be followed by an example of how the teacher might actually **model** the procedure for students. It is believed that after the discussion and illustration of how to **model** the procedure for students, the teacher will be able to use Form B for individual evaluation.

A Discussion of Prediction and Retelling Procedures

Classroom Environment

Some students may not become involved easily in making predictions and retelling stories, even after the teacher models the procedure. If students are not sure of what to say or do, teachers may need to base their lessons on student experiences and social activities. The teacher should emphasize that a student's willingness to try is of utmost importance.

Predicting and Retelling

The teacher should consider the following:

> Develop themes or topics based on the age and interests of students (young students, animals or pets, older students, T.V. shows or the circus).
> Use a variety of instructional groupings: small groups, whole class, or pairs.
> During this preparation period students will need similar copies of stories and titles. Pictures might be included in the copy or placed on the chalkboard.
> During the predicting part, have students use only the title and picture.

Steps in the Predicting and Retelling Preparation Period

Predicting: (Allow approximately five minutes for predicting.)

Step 1　Using title and picture, ask students to predict the plot or problem. Initially ask them to work in pairs. Each pair of students can elect to write or discuss their responses. If they do write responses, do not collect the papers.

Step 2　Ask students to report their predictions. Record the predictions on the chalkboard, and discuss them. Predictions might be about plot, problem, or words in the title. Tell students they will come back to their predictions after they have had an opportunity to hear the selection read by the teacher and have read it themselves.

Retelling: (Allow approximately ten minutes for retelling.)

Step 3　Students are to follow the selection as the teacher reads it aloud. After the teacher completes the selection, the teacher should ask the students to read the selection silently. Again, it is more important for the student to understand the selection than it is for the student to memorize the selection.

Step 4　Go back to step one, and discuss the various student predictions, not on the basis of correct or incorrect (good or bad) responses but rather on how "close" the predictions were or the "fun" of making predictions.

The above steps merely outline the procedures used during prediction and retelling. What follows is an example of how to **introduce** these procedures in a lesson where the teacher is asked to **model** these procedures for students.

Teacher as Model

Find a simple selection. The selection should have a picture and title. The picture could be a drawing on the chalkboard or an actual picture. The title must be large enough to be seen by students.

Show the picture and title. The teacher might make several predictions about what **he or she thinks the story or selection** will be about. Thus the teacher is modeling what the students are expected to do later.

Here is an example of a simple second grade selection:

Find a picture of a bean seed (picture file or encyclopedia)

Title: *From Little Seed to Big Plants*

Predicting: Teacher—"I think that this story is a real or true story. The picture shows a bean seed, and I know that seeds grow into plants. The story might be about how seeds grow into plants (that is my prediction or guess)."

Selection: (teacher reads aloud to students)

"What is in a seed?" asked Betty.
Betty's brother gave her a big bean and said, "Cut this open and see."
Betty cut the bean open. She found a baby plant in the bean.
Betty asked her brother if another bean seed would grow if she planted it.
Betty planted the seed and watered it every day.
When Betty saw the first plant leaves, she wanted to show them to everyone.

Retelling: Teacher—"The main *characters* are Betty and her older brother. I think Betty was about seven years old. Her brother might have been in high school. (*Problem*) Betty wanted to know what was in a seed. This led Betty to actually grow the seed. I think Betty's brother helped her learn about seeds and how they grow. (*Outcome*) Betty saw the little plant in the seed. After she grew the seed, she learned that little seeds grow into big plants. I know that Betty was proud of her plant because she wanted to show everybody her new bean plant."

Note: The teacher never asked the students to predict or retell any part of the title or selection. The teacher did everything possible to **model** the procedure for students.

It is believed that the above procedure is one way to prepare students for Form B Evaluation. What follows are the two purposes for Form B and a discussion of each of these two purposes.

Purposes for Form B

To evaluate the student's ability to make predictions and retell the story or selection.
To read comfortably at some level of graded difficulty.

Form B requires students to predict before reading and retell after reading. Form B uses what the author calls **scorable parts** to evaluate the students ability to predict and retell. These scorable parts are:

predicting—the use of pictures and title to anticipate selection content
character(s)—the use of character(s) to deal with the essential elements of the story
problems—those elements used by the character(s) to identify problems or reach goals
outcome—usually the character(s) solution to the problem or the attainment of the goal

How these **scorable parts** are used and marked will be introduced on pages 17–19.

Prompting (to obtain predicting and retelling responses). If the student is providing only limited responses to the suggested predicting and retelling questions, the teacher should prompt the student. If the student **needs help,** it seems reasonable to assume that the student is having difficulty with some or all aspects of **predicting and retelling.** Mark the following on the Inventory Record for Teachers for each level:

Prompting:
very little _____
average _____
needs help _____

The second purpose is designed to enable the teacher to find quickly a comfortable reading level for each student. FORM B uses the following simple check list for each grade selection to determine comfortable reading levels.

> Comfortable Reading Level
> -fluent (above _____ ave _____ below _____)

The teacher should quickly check the above list **during** or **after** the student reads orally the selections in Form B. Fluency and/or very little prompting suggests that the student pronounces words well, observes punctuation marks, and in general is comfortable with the selection. Therefore, the **Comfortable Reading Level** is the level at which the student should be able to "process words" with little difficulty. If the student lacks fluency, it seems reasonable to assume that the reading material is too difficult.

Form B selections are based on graded reading levels. For example, the selection entitled "A Fish for Sale" is believed to be typical of the type of material found in most second grade reading programs. Therefore, if the student can read comfortably at level two, the teacher might assume that the student is able to read most second level material.

Allow me to briefly review the two purposes for Form B:

Purpose 1 is met when the teacher uses the four scorable parts to assess the student's ability to predict and retell stories.

Purpose 2 is met when the student demonstrates the ability to read comfortably at some level of reading difficulty.

Helpful Hints When Using Form B

1. The aim is to find out if the student understands the story or selection.
2. If the student seems to have the ability to predict and retell the story, **do not interrupt** with guided questions. Strive for a free flow of information.
3. The questions used in the story guide, at each grade level, are merely suggestions. Feel free to modify or rephrase them.
4. Take notes or use key words when student is predicting and retelling (use lines provided on the Informal Record Form). It is important to reduce the delay or interferences. Some teachers might like to tape the student's responses to review the student's retelling at a later time. However, tape recording takes time, and you may not want to use it.

Form B Administration and Interpretation

What follows is a complete example of how to administer and interpret FORM B. This example includes:

1. Suggested dialog for **getting started** with an individual student.
2. A sample Inventory Record for Teachers giving responses of a second grade student named **Joan.**
3. A sample Inventory Record—Summary Sheet (for Joan) prepared by the author to illustrate how to use and interpret Form B.

Form B INVENTORY RECORD SUMMARY SHEET

Student's Name ___JOAN___ Grade __2__ Age __7-4__
Date __May 199-__ School __WOOD__ Administered by __N.J. SILVAROLI__
(yr) (mo)

PREDICTION - RETELLING

Level	Prediction	Character(s)	Problem	Outcome	Total
1					
2	4	5	5	5	19
3	4	2	2	2	10
4					
5					
6					

PROMPTING

Very little	Ave	Needs help
X		
		X

COMFORTABLE READING LEVEL

Above	Ave	Below
X		
	X	

Summary of Specific Instructional Needs:

Ability to Predict: _Joan understands and is willing to make predictions._

Ability to Retell: _At the 2nd level she appears to comprehend the selection. However, at the 3rd level she needs help with characters, problems and outcomes._

Prompting to obtain predicting and retelling responses: _Considerable prompting was needed at the 3rd level._

Comments: _Joan needs specific retelling instruction and practice at the 2nd level. Joan appears to be an average reader for her age and grade level._

Comfortable Reading Level: _She seems comfortable with 2nd level reading material._

Form B, Level 2

FISH FOR SALE

Susan got ten fish and a tank for her birthday.
She loved the fish and learned to take good care of them.
One day Susan saw six new baby fish in the tank.
The fish tank was too small for all of the fish.
Dad said he would buy another tank for the baby fish.
Everyone began giving Susan fish and equipment.
Soon she had tanks for big fish, small fish, and baby fish.

Each tank had water plants, air tubes, and stones on the bottom.
Mom said, "Enough! Susan your room looks like a store for fish."
That gave Susan an idea.
Why not put all of the fish tanks in the garage and put up a sign?
Susan and her Dad moved everything into the garage.
Susan made a big sign that read, "FISH FOR SALE."

Student Responses

Low   High (circle number)

PREDICTION: **Picture and Title**   1 2 3 ④ 5
What do you think is meant by the title, "Fish for Sale?" What do you think the story will be about?

A kid wants to buy a fish. The fish are on sale.

Retelling:
CHARACTERS   1 2 3 4 ⑤
What do you remember about the people in the story?

Susan got a fish for her birthday. The fish had baby fish - six I think the story said.

Problem   1 2 3 4 ⑤
What was the problem? What would you do if you had this problem?

Too many fish. Susan needed more tanks. Susan's mother was upset (why did her mother get upset?) The room was messy. I'd keep the room clean.

OUTCOME   1 2 3 4 ⑤
How was the problem solved? What do you think Susan's goal was?

Susan and her Dad moved the fish tanks to the garage. Susan got the idea to make a sign and sell the fish.

TOTAL SCORE _19_   SCORING GUIDE: **Second**   **Prompting:**

(16 to 20	Comprehension excellent)	very little _X_
6 to 15	Needs assistance	average _____
5 or less	Too difficult	needs help _____

Inventory Record for Teachers, Form B

Form B, Level 3

THE FOX – A FARMER'S FRIEND

"Meg, look! That's a female fox ready to have cubs." Uncle Mike was excited,"I haven't seen a fox around here for ten years." Meg said "Shall I get your gun?" "There's no need for a gun," Uncle Mike replied. "Foxes help farmers by eating pests like mice, squirrels, frogs, and insects."

The next day Meg and her uncle were unhappy to learn that some farmers were hunting for the fox. These farmers didn't believe that a fox was helpful. Foxes save the farmers' crops by eating pests that destroy their crops. The farmers were sure that foxes only killed their chickens and other small animals.

After weeks of hunting, the farmers gave up trying to kill the fox. When Uncle Mike and Meg found fresh fox and cub tracks on the far end of their farm, they were happy.

Student Responses

	Low	High

PREDICTION: Picture and Title   1 2 3 ④ 5

Have you ever seen a fox? If no, discuss things about a fox. What do you think the story will be about?

(Joan had seen a fox in the zoo.) A fox wandered around the woods. It went to this farm house. The farmer keep the fox for a "watch dog."

Retelling:

CHARACTERS   1 ② 3 4 5

What can you tell me about the people in the story?

Uncle Mike was a good man. The kid... I can't remember his name... was nice – can't remember anymore.

Problem   1 ② 3 4 5

The fox had a problem. What do think was happening? Why do you think Meg and Uncle Mike worried?

Hunters wanted to kill the fox. (why did they want to kill the fox?) I don't know. (Why were the kid and Uncle Mike worried?) I don't know.

OUTCOME   1 ② 3 4 5

What happened to the fox? When Uncle Mike and Meg saw the tracks, what did they learn? How did Uncle Mike and Meg feel?

The fox didn't get killed. The hunters gave up. (How do you know that the fox didn't get killed?) I guessed – That's all I know.

TOTAL SCORE ____

SCORING GUIDE: Third

16 to 20	Comprehension excellent
6 to 15	Needs assistance
5 or less	Too difficult

Prompting:

very little _____

average _____

needs help _X_

Inventory Record for Teachers, Form B

1. Getting started dialog:

Silvaroli:	"Joan, if I use words like predict or prediction, do you know what I mean?"
Joan:	"No."
Silvaroli:	"How about words like guess or making guesses?"
Joan:	"Yes, because I know how to guess."
Silvaroli:	"O.K., Let's practice making a guess. What do you think the cafeteria is having for lunch today?"
Joan:	"I don't know."
Silvaroli:	"O.K., but you said that you knew how to guess. How about making a guess? You don't have to be right. All you need to do is make a guess."
Joan:	"I think they are having hamburgers."
Silvaroli:	"How will you actually know if they are having hamburgers?"
Joan:	"When I go to lunch."
Silvaroli:	"Joan, you made a good guess. Let's make more guesses now. I'm going to show you a **picture** and the **title of a story,** and I would like you to make guesses about what the story might be about."

Note: Joan was in second grade; therefore, I selected the second level selection titled "A Fish For Sale."

2. A sample Inventory Record—Summary Sheet (for Joan) prepared by the author (p. 17).
3. A sample Inventory Record for Teachers giving Joan's responses (pp. 18–19).

Summary for Individual Evaluation

Step 1   Rapport. Make the student comfortable. Complete top of FORM B INVENTORY RECORD—SUMMARY SHEET (p. 82). Record the student's name, grade, age, date, school, and who administered Form B. (See p. 14 for getting started with an individual student.)

Step 2   Begin selections at the level of the student's current grade level, that is, begin a third grader at the third grade selection ("The Fox—A Farmer's Friend"). If the student has the ability to predict and retell and is reading comfortably, go on to the fourth level. If the student is having difficulty, move back to the second level. However, if you have reason to believe that the student is reading above or below grade level, adjust the starting level accordingly.

Step 3   Ask the student to look at the picture as you read the title orally (cover the selection while reading title). Using the picture and title, ask the student to **predict** (make guesses about the selection). If necessary, prompt the student without giving away the story.

Step 4   Ask the student to read the selection orally. Check responses on the Comfortable Reading Level Chart (Above, Ave., or Below), as or after the student reads. Transfer this information to the Inventory Record Summary Sheet.

Step 5   After the student has read the selection orally, ask the student to **retell** the story by noting character(s), problems, and outcome. The guided questions listed for the predicting and retelling scorable areas are merely **suggested questions. Feel free to change the questions as needed.**

Step 6   **If necessary prompt** the student in such a way as to not give away the story. If the student needs considerable help (prompting) it is assumed that the student is having difficulty comprehending what he or she is reading.

Step 7   As previously stated: **Comfortable Reading Level** is designed to estimate the level at which the student is able to read **without** difficulty; **Scorable parts total and prompting** are designed to estimate how well the student comprehends what he or she is reading.

Step 8   Transfer the comfortable reading level, scorable parts total, and prompting information from the Inventory Record for Teachers to the Inventory Record—Summary Sheet.

S P E C I F I C   I N S T R U C T I O N S

For Administering Forms C and D
(To Be Used by Junior High School Students,
High School Students, and Adults)

Part 1   Graded Word Lists   *Form C and Form D*

Purpose   To identify specific word recognition errors and to estimate the approximate starting level at which the mature student begins reading the Graded Paragraphs in Part 2.

Procedure   Present the Graded Word Lists, starting at Level 1, and say:

"Pronounce each word. If you are not sure, or do not know the word, then say what you think it is."

Discontinue at the level at which the student mispronounces or does not know five of the twenty words in a particular grade level (75 percent). Each correct response is worth five points.

As the student pronounces the words at each level, the teacher should record all word responses on the Inventory Record for Teachers.[9] Self-corrected errors are counted as acceptable responses in Part 1. These recorded word responses may by analyzed later to determine specific word recognition needs.

Sample

1	her	<u>his</u>	(error)
2	fire	<u>+</u>	
3	frog	<u>DK</u> (don't know)	(error)
4	garden	<u>+</u>	

After the student reaches the cut-off point (75) percent, the oral reading level should be started at the highest level at which the student successfully pronounced all twenty words (100 percent) in the list.

9. The Inventory Record for Teachers is a separate record form printed on standard 8 1/2-by-11 inch paper. Note: teachers have the publisher's permission to reproduce all, or any part, of the inventory record for teachers, Form C, pp. 107–117 and Form D, pp. 137–147.

Part 2 Graded Paragraphs *Form C and Form D*

Purposes:
1. To estimate the student's independent and instructional reading levels. If necessary estimate the student's frustration and listening capacity levels.
2. To identify significant word recognition errors made during oral reading and to estimate the extent to which the student actually comprehends what he or she reads.

Levels[10]

Four levels may be identified through the use of the Classroom Reading Inventory. However, most classroom teachers are concerned with independent and instructional levels. Teachers do this in order to reduce testing and scoring time.

Independent Level
Instructional Level
Frustration Level
Listening Capacity Level

Procedure: Present the Graded Paragraphs, starting at the highest level at which the student recognized all twenty words in the word list, Part 1. Ask the student to read the story out loud. Tell the student that you will ask several questions when he or she has finished.

Background Knowledge Assessment

Before the student is asked to read the story, the teacher should quickly assess the student's background knowledge. Each story in the CRI begins with a leading discussion statement called Background Knowledge Assessment. If the student has some knowledge of the selection to be read, check the box marked adequate, and continue. If the student has little or no background knowledge, substitute a selection from Form D (if you're using Form C).

Discontinue the Graded Paragraphs as soon as the student experiences frustration with either word recognition or comprehension.

10. See page 8 for a discussion of Reading Levels for Forms A, C, and D.

CRI INTERPRETATION

For Forms A, C and D

The Classroom Reading Inventory is designed to provide the teacher with a realistic estimate of the student's independent, instructional, frustration, and listening capacity levels in reading. However, merely identifying various reading levels is only slightly better than classifying the student on the basis of a norm-referenced test score.

The Classroom Reading Inventory is much more effective when the teacher is able to pinpoint consistent errors in word recognition and/or comprehension development. The Classroom Reading Inventory should enable the teacher to answer these specific questions:

Is the student having more difficulty with word recognition or comprehension skills?

Does the student have equal difficulty with both word recognition and comprehension skills?

If the student's difficulty is in the area of word recognition skills, are the problems with consonants, vowels, or syllables?

If the student's difficulty is comprehension, are the problems with fact, inference, or vocabulary questions? Is he or she a word caller?

Does the student appear to have other needs? Does the student appear to need glasses? Does the student appear to be anxious or withdrawn? Are high-interest/low vocabulary reading materials needed?

Following are a sample CRI record and a CRI practice work sheet. These examples are designed to help the teacher gain information on the scoring and interpretation of the Classroom Reading Inventory. Such information should enable the teacher to deal effectively with the type of questions presented above.

Sample CRI Record

Pamela T. is a fifth-grade student whose chronological age is ten years, six months. Her full scale I.Q., as measured by the Wechsler Intelligence Scale for Children-Revised is 98, giving Pamela a mental age of ten years, four months. In her class, Pamela is in the middle reading group. Her grade equivalency score in reading is 4.8, as measured by a group reading achievement test.

Pamela's teacher Wilbur Millston administered Form A of the Classroom Reading Inventory to Pamela. Her Inventory Record and Summary Sheet follow on pages 24–30.

Form A Inventory Record

Summary Sheet

Student's Name __Pamela T.__   Grade __5__   Age (Chronological) __10-6__
                                                                      yrs. mos.
Date __2/15/94__   School __Central__   Administered by __W. Millston__

Part 1 — Word Lists			Part 2 — Graded Paragraphs			
Grade Level	Percent of Words Correct	Word Recognition Errors		SIG WR	Comp	L.C.
		Consonants	PP			
PP	100	____ consonants	P			
1 P	100	____ blends	1	IND	IND	
1	100	____ digraphs	2 →	IND	INST	
		____ endings	3	IND	FRUST	
		____ compounds	4			
		____ contractions	5			
		Vowels	6			
		____ long	7			
		____ short	8			
		____ long/short oo				
2	100	____ vowel + r				
		____ diphthong				
		____ vowel comb.				
		____ a + 1 or w				
		Syllable				
3	95	____ visual patterns				
4	95	____ prefix				
		____ suffix				
5	95	**Word Recognition reinforcement and Vocabulary development**				
6	75					

Estimated Levels

	Grade
Independent	1
Instructional	2 (range)
Frustration	3
Listening Capacity	Not Determined

Comp Errors

_____ Factual (F)
✓ Inference (I)
✓ Vocabulary (V)
✓ "Word Caller"
(A student who reads without associating meaning)
_____ Poor Memory

Summary of Specific Needs:

Comprehension problems. Needs help associating her experience with print. Pam also needs help with Inference (I) and Vocabulary (V) questions.

Permission is granted by the publisher to reproduce pp. 24 through 30.

Form A   Part 1   Graded Word Lists

PP		**P**		**1**		**2**	
1 this	+	1 came	+	1 new	+	1 birthday	+
2 her	+	2 day	+	2 leg	+	2 free	+
3 about	+	3 up	+	3 feet	+	3 isn't	+
4 to	+	4 was	+	4 hear	+	4 beautiful	+
5 and	+	5 after	+	5 food	+	5 job	+
6 it	+	6 now	+	6 learn	+	6 elephant	+
7 he	+	7 read	+	7 hat	+	7 cowboy	+
8 for	+	8 other	+	8 ice	+	8 branch	+
9 like	+	9 went	+	9 letter	+	9 asleep	+
10 can	+	10 just	+	10 green	+	10 mice	+
11 big	___	11 play	___	11 outside	___	11 corn	___
12 said	___	12 many	___	12 happy	___	12 baseball	___
13 house	___	13 trees	___	13 less	___	13 garden	___
14 look	___	14 time	___	14 drop	___	14 hall	___
15 go	___	15 good	___	15 stopping	___	15 pet	___
16 see	___	16 into	___	16 grass	___	16 blows	___
17 there	___	17 we	___	17 street	___	17 gray	___
18 little	___	18 something	___	18 page	___	18 law	___
19 is	___	19 what	___	19 ever	___	19 bat	___
20 all	___	20 saw	___	20 let's	___	20 guess	___
_100_ %		_100_ %		_100_ %		_100_ %	

Teacher note: If the child misses five words in any column—stop Part 1. Begin Graded Paragraphs, Part 2 (Form A), at the highest level in which the child recognized all 20 words. To save time, if the first ten words were correct, go on to the next list. If one of the words were missed, continue the entire list.

3		**4**		**5**		**6**	
1 distant	+	1 unhappy	+	1 moan	*man*	1 brisk	*brisk*
2 phone	+	2 jug	+	2 hymn	+	2 nostrils	*DK*
3 turkeys	+	3 innocent	+	3 bravely	+	3 marsh	+
4 crunch	+	4 relax	+	4 dispose	+	4 headlight	+
5 chief	+	5 bound	+	5 shrill	+	5 calmly	+
6 foolish	+	6 seventeen	+	6 jewel	+	6 farthest	+
7 engage	*enrage*	7 disturb	+	7 loudly	+	7 wreath	*wrath*
8 glow	+	8 glove	+	8 register	+	8 emptiness	+
9 drain	+	9 compass	+	9 embarrass	+	9 billows	+
10 fully	+	10 attractive	+	10 graceful	+	10 knight	+
11 crowd	+	11 impact	+	11 cube	+	11 instinct	+
12 energy	+	12 lettuce	+	12 scarf	+	12 harpoon	+
13 passenger	+	13 operator	+	13 muffled	+	13 pounce	+
14 shark	+	14 regulation	*regulate*	14 pacing	+	14 rumor	+
15 vacation	+	15 violet	+	15 oars	+	15 dazzle	+
16 pencil	+	16 settlers	+	16 biblical	+	16 combustion	+
17 goodness	+	17 merrily	+	17 thermometer	+	17 hearth	*DK*
18 discover	+	18 internal	+	18 zone	+	18 mockingbird	+
19 polite	+	19 drama	+	19 salmon	+	19 ridiculous	*redeck-*
20 nail	+	20 landscape	+	20 magical	+	20 widen	+
	95 %		*95* %		*95* %		*75* %

Background Knowledge Assessment: This story is about puppies. What can you tell me about puppies?

adequate ☒   inadequate ☐

Puppies

Puppies are fun to watch.

They are born with their eyes closed.

Their ears are closed, too.

This is why they use their touch and smell.

Puppies open their eyes and ears after two weeks.

By four weeks most puppies can bark.

Puppies grow up to make good pets.

Comprehension Check

(F) 1. _+_ When puppies are born, are their eyes open or closed?   (closed)

(F) 2. _≠_ At birth, puppies must use their touch and smell. Why?
(eyes closed or ears closed)

(F) 3. _+_ How long does it take for puppies to open their eyes and ears?   (2 weeks)

(F) 4. _+_ What can puppies do after 4 weeks? (Bark)

(I) 5. _½_ Why do you think puppies are fun to watch?   (they jump, run around, roll around)

They can bark

Scoring Guide   First

SIG WR Errors		Comp Errors	
IND	0	IND	0 - 1
INST	2	INST	1 1/2 - 2
FRUST	4+	FRUST	2 1/2+

Background Knowledge Assessment: This story tells how to make a simple telephone. How often do you use the telephone?   adequate ☒   inadequate ☐

A Simple Telephone

You can make your own private telephone.

You will need two empty tin cans and

some string. The two cans must have the

tops cut off. Punch a small hole in the

bottom of each can. Push the string

through the holes and tie the string ends

in a knot. Give someone a can and ask

them to move away. The string must be

P

straight and tight. One of you should

speak into the open end of the "telephone."

The other person will hear the voice as it

moves along the string. Now you have a

"simple telephone."

Comprehension Check

(F) 1. _+_ Name two things you need to make a simple telephone.   (cans and string)

(F) 2. _+_ What do you need to do to the cans? (cut tops off and / or punch a hole in bottoms)

(I) 3. _+_ Why do you have to tie knots in the string?   (so string won't slip out of can)

(I) 4. _✓_ Why should the string be straight and tight? (so voice can move along string)   *Don't know*

(I) 5. _½_ Why do you think two people must be far away from each other when they talk on the "phone"? (they can hear each other without the phone)

easy to talk

Scoring Guide   Second

SIG WR Errors		Comp Errors	
IND	2	IND	0 - 1
INST	5	INST	1 1/2 - 2
FRUST	10	FRUST	2 1/2+

Form A   Part 2/Level 3 (96 Words)

Background Knowledge Assessment: What can you tell me about elephants?

adequate ☒   inadequate ☐

Strange Facts About Elephants

Elephants are unusual animals. They take

showers by shooting a stream of water

from their trunks. An elephant uses its

trunk to carry heavy logs. Elephants also

use their trunks to breathe, smell, and eat.

A frightened elephant can run at a speed

of more than 25 miles per hour. On a long

journey an elephant travels at about 10 miles

per hour. The gray skin of an elephant

looks thick and strong. It's not— flies and

other insects can bite into the skin.

When you go to the zoo, be sure to visit

the elephants.

Comprehension Check

(F) 1. _+_ Tell two of the ways elephants use
their trunks. (shoot) water,
breathe, smell, eat (carry logs)

(F) 2. ✓ If frightened, an elephant can run at
what speed?   (25 m.p.h.)
Don't know

(I) 3. ✓ The skin of an elephant is not as
strong as it looks. Why do we
think this is?   (flies and insects
can bite into the skin) *Don't
know*

(F) 4. _+_ How fast do elephants travel on
long trips? (10 m.p.h.)

(V) 5. ½ What does the word journey mean?
(a long trip, travel)
to go   —?

Scoring Guide   Third

SIG WR Errors   Comp Errors

IND	2	IND	0 - 1
INST	5	INST	1 1/2 - 2
FRUST	10	FRUST	2 1/2⁺

Upon examination of Part 2 (Graded Paragraphs), it appears that Pamela's problem is with comprehension. She seems to have difficulty with inference and vocabulary questions. There is no problem with word recognition skills. Pamela might be called a word caller. She can sound out almost any word presented to her. However, she does not associate meaning with the words she decodes.

Again, if you are unfamiliar with how children develop comprehension skills in reading or what is meant by the term *word caller,* it is recommended that you refer to the textbook by Searfoss and Readence, *Helping Children Learn to Read.*[11]

Note: Pamela began the Classroom Reading Inventory by responding to the Graded Word Lists in Part 1. Mr. Millston began part 2 (Graded Paragraphs) at the last place Pamela had 100 percent, which was Level 2.

If Pamela had obtained IND in both WR and COMP, her teacher would go on to the Level 3 paragraph. Pamela was IND in WR, and INST in COMP; therefore, her teacher dropped back to the point where IND was reached for both WR and COMP (primer reading level). Level 3 is Pamela's instructional level.

Teacher note: The Graded Paragraphs were started at Level 2. This was the last level at which Pamela T. successfully pronounced all twenty words (100 percent) on Part 1, Graded Word List. She evidenced comprehension difficulty; therefore, lower levels of Graded Paragraphs were used.

What follows is a practice exercise for Linda P. Linda P. is a third-grade student whose chronological age is nine years, three months. Her Inventory Record has been partially completed. Parts 1 and 2, Estimated Levels, Consistent Word Recognition Errors, Consistent Comprehension Errors, and Summary of Specific Needs have been left blank. Analyze the Classroom Reading Inventory for Form A, Parts 1 and 2, located on pages 3–6. Complete her Summary Sheet and compare your responses with the author's responses on page 30.

---

11. Searfoss and Readence, *Helping Children Learn to Read,* 3rd Edition, Allyn & Bacon, 1994.

Form A Inventory Record _____

Summary Sheet (Sample Exercises[12])

Student's Name _____ *Linda P.* _____ Grade ___3___ Age (Chronological) __9-3__

yrs. mos.

Date _____ School _____ Administered by _____

Part 1 Word Lists			Part 2 Graded Paragraphs			
Grade Level	Percent of Words Correct	Word Recognition Errors		SIG WR	Comp	L.C.
		Consonants	PP			
PP	_____	___ consonants	P			
1 P	_____	___ blends	1			
1	_____	___ digraphs	2			
		___ endings	3			
		___ compounds	4			
		___ contractions	5			
		Vowels	6			
		___ long	7			
		___ short	8			
		___ long / short oo				
2	_____	___ vowel + r				
		___ diphthong	**Estimated Levels**			
		___ vowel comb.				
		___ a + 1 or w			Grade	
		Syllable	Independent		___	
3	_____	___ visual patterns	Instructional		___ (range)	
4	_____	___ prefix	Frustration		___	
		___ suffix	Listening Capacity		___	
5	_____	Word Recognition reinforcement and Vocabulary development				
6	_____					

Comp Errors	Summary of Specific Needs:
_____ Factual (F)	
_____ Inference (I)	
_____ Vocabulary (V)	
_____ "Word Caller" (A student who reads without associating meaning)	
_____ Poor Memory	

Permission is granted by the publisher to reproduce pp. 59 through 70.

12. Answer the questions on p. 37 after completing Linda P's Summary Sheet.

Form A   Part 1   Graded Word Lists

PP		P		1		2	
1 this	+	1 came	+	1 new	+	1 birthday	+
2 her	+	2 day	+	2 leg	legs	2 free	+
3 about	+	3 up	+	3 feet	+	3 isn't	+
4 to	+	4 was	+	4 hear	+	4 beautiful	+
5 and	+	5 after	+	5 food	+	5 job	+
6 it	+	6 now	+	6 learn	+	6 elephant	+
7 he	+	7 read	+	7 hat	+	7 cowboy	cow–
8 for	+	8 other	DK	8 ice	+	8 branch	+
9 like	+	9 went	+	9 letter	+	9 asleep	+
10 can	+	10 just	+	10 green	DK	10 mice	+
11 big	___	11 play	+	11 outside	out –	11 corn	+
12 said	___	12 many	+	12 happy	+	12 baseball	+
13 house	___	13 trees	+	13 less	+	13 garden	grade
14 look	___	14 time	+	14 drop	+	14 hall	+
15 go	___	15 good	+	15 stopping	+	15 pet	+
16 see	___	16 into	+	16 grass	+	16 blows	bilow
17 there	___	17 we	+	17 street	say	17 gray	gay
18 little	___	18 something	+	18 page	+	18 law	+
19 is	___	19 what	+	19 ever	+	19 bat	but
20 all	___	20 saw	+	20 let's	+	20 guess	+
	_100_ %		_95_ %		_80_ %		_75_ %

Teacher note: If the child misses five words in any column, stop Part 1. Begin Graded Paragraphs, Part 2 (Form A), at the highest level in which the child recognized all 20 words. To save time, if the first ten words were correct, go on to the next list. If one of the words was missed, continue the entire list.

Form A   Part 2/Level PP (24 Words)

Background Knowledge Assessment:[13] This story is about two children and their play car. Tell me what you think the children are doing.   adequate ☒   inadequate ☐

The Play Car

"See my play car," said Tom.

"It can go fast."

Ann said, "It's a big car."

"Yes," said Tom.

"Would you like a ride?"

Comprehension Check

(F) 1. ＋ What are the names of the boy and girl in the story?   (Tom and Ann)

(F) 2. ＋ What were they talking about? (The play car, etc.)

(F) 3. ＋ Who owned the car? (Tom)

(F) 4. ＋ What did Ann (the girl) say about the car?   (Big car)

(I) 5. ＋ Tell one thing that Tom might have liked about the car.   (It was fast, big.)

Scoring Guide   Preprimer

SIG WR Errors		Comp Errors	
IND	0	IND	0 - 1
INST	1-2	INST	1 1/2 - 2
FRUST	3+	FRUST	2 1/2+

Form A   Part 2/Level P (39 Words)

Background Knowledge Assessment: Has your class ever taken a field trip? What can you tell about field trips?   adequate ☒   inadequate ☐

Our Bus Ride

It was time to go to the farm.

"Get in the bus," said Mrs. Brown.

"We are ready to go now."

The children climbed into the bus.

Away went the bus.

It was a good day for a ride.

Comprehension Check

(F) 1. ＋ Where were they going? (Farm)

(F) 2. ＋ How were they going? (By bus)

(I) 3. ＋ Who was Mrs. Brown? (Teacher, or bus driver)

(F) 4. ＋ How did the children know that it was time for the bus to leave?   (Mrs. Brown said, "We are ready to go now."

(F) 5. ＋ Was this bus ride taking place during the day or at night?   (Day)

Scoring Guide   Preprimer

SIG WR Errors		Comp Errors	
IND	0	IND	0 - 1
INST	2	INST	1 1/2 - 2
FRUST	4+	FRUST	2 1/2+

---

13. See page 5 for a discussion of Background Knowledge Assessment.

Background Knowledge Assessment: This story is about puppies. What can you tell me about puppies?   adequate [X]   inadequate [ ]

Puppies

Puppies are fun to watch.

They are born with their eyes closed.
(P above "born")

Their ears are closed, too.

This is why they use their touch and
smell.
(P above "smell")

Puppies open their eyes and ears after
two weeks.

By four weeks most puppies can bark.

little
∧ Puppies grow up to make good pets.

Comprehension Check

(F) 1. ⊥ When puppies are born, are their eyes
        open or closed?   (closed)

(F) 2. ⊥ At birth, puppies must use their touch
        and smell. Why?
        (eyes closed or ears closed)

(F) 3. ⊥ How long does it take for puppies to
        open their eyes and ears?   (2 weeks)

(F) 4. ✓ What can puppies do after 4 weeks?
        (Bark)   *walk*

(I) 5. ⊥ Why do you think puppies are fun to
        watch?   (they jump, run around,
        roll around)

        *they run and jump
        funny*

Scoring Guide   First

SIG WR Errors		Comp Errors	
IND	0	IND	0 - 1
INST	2	INST	1 1/2 - 2
FRUST	4⁺	FRUST	2 1/2⁺

(INST 2 circled in SIG WR Errors; IND 0-1 circled in Comp Errors)

Background Knowledge Assessment: This story tells how to make a simple telephone.
How often do you use the telephone?   adequate [✗]   inadequate [ ]

A Simple Telephone

You can make your own private telephone. *[P] phone*

You will need two empty (tin) cans and some *[P]* string. The two cans must have the tops cut off. Punch a small hole in the bottom *near* of each can. Push the *small* string through (the) (holes) and tie the string ends in a knot.

Give someone a can and ask them to move (away.) The string must be straight and *[P]* tight. One of you should speak into the open end of the "telephone." The other *phone* person will hear the voice as it moves along the string. Now you have a "simple telephone." *phone*

Comprehension Check

(F) 1. _+_ Name two things you need to make a
    simple telephone.   (cans and string)

(F) 2. _+_ What do you need to do to the cans?
    (cut tops off and / or punch a hole in
    bottoms)

(I) 3. _+_ Why do you have to tie knots in the
    string?   (so string won't slip out
    of can)

(I) 4. _✓_ Why should the string be straight and
    tight? (so voice can move along
    string)   *Don't know*

(I) 5. _✓_ Why do you think two people must be
    far away from each other when they
    talk on the "phone"? (they can hear
    each other without the phone)
    not sure

Scoring Guide   Second

SIG WR Errors		Comp Errors	
IND	2	IND	0 - 1
INST	5	(INST	1 1/2 - 2)
(FRUST	10)	FRUST	2 1/2+

Form A Inventory Record

Summary Sheet

Student's Name __Linda P.__   Grade __3__ Age (Chronological) __9-3__ yrs. mos.

Date _____   School _____   Administered by __N. Silvaroli__

Part 1 Word Lists			Part 2 Graded Paragraphs			
Grade Level	Percent of Words Correct	Word Recognition Errors		SIG WR	Comp	L.C.
PP	100	**Consonants** ___ consonants ✓ blends ___ digraphs ✓ endings ✓ compounds ✓ contractions	PP	IND	IND	
1 P	95		P	IND	IND	
1	80		1	INST	IND	
			2	FRUST	INST	
		Vowels ___ long ___ short ___ long/short oo	3			
			4			
			5			
2	75	___ vowel + r ___ diphthong ___ vowel comb. ___ a + 1 or w	6			
			7			
			8			

Estimated Levels

	Grade
Independent	P
Instructional	I (range)
Frustration	2
Listening Capacity	Not Determined

Syllable
___ visual patterns
___ prefix
___ suffix

Word Recognition reinforcement and Vocabulary development

(Grade Level rows: 3, 4, 5, 6 — percent blank)

Comp Errors
_____ Factual (F)
_____ Inference (I)
_____ Vocabulary (V)
_____ "Word Caller"
  (A student who reads without asso-
  ciating meaning)
_____ Poor Memory

Summary of Specific Needs:

See paragraph below for discussion of Linda's reading needs.

Linda is having difficulty applying word recognition skills. She appears to understand consonants and digraphs but needs to learn to apply the remainder of the consonant, vowel, and syllable skills. Linda comprehends what she reads but might experience difficulty with inference questions. She has an independent (IND) level of primer (P). Therefore, she should be encouraged to read independently at this level.

Answer the following questions:[14]

1. Significant WR Errors are determined from student responses on Part 1, Graded Word Lists or Part 2 Graded Paragraphs? _____
2. Why were the words from 11 to 20, Part 1, PP skipped? _____
3. Given Linda's responses on Part 1, what is the beginning starting level on Part 2? _____
4. Linda's background knowledge for the "Play Car" selection appears to be adequate. What should the teacher do?
5. Discuss the significant and insignificant WR Errors in the selection Part 2, Level 2.
6. The Level 2 selection has 97 words. Is the title included in the word count? _____

14. See page 38 for answers to these six questions.

Answers for six questions on page 37:

1. Part 2, Graded Paragraphs
2. Words 11–20 are as difficult as 1–10, therefore, skipping them saves time.
3. Last place she had 100 percent on Part 1, therefore, PP Level.
4. Mark adequate and ask her to read the selection.
5. Needing assistance (P) with the words **born** and **smell** interfered with syntactical structure. Inserting and repeating were not significant because these errors did not interfere with Linda's fluency or thought process.
6. No, title not included in total words.

F O R M   A

Part 1 Graded Word Lists

Form A   Graded Word Lists

1 this	1 came
2 her	2 day
3 about	3 up
4 to	4 was
5 and	5 after
6 it	6 now
7 he	7 read
8 for	8 other
9 like	9 went
10 can	10 just
11 big	11 play
12 said	12 many
13 house	13 trees
14 look	14 time
15 go	15 good
16 see	16 into
17 there	17 we
18 little	18 something
19 is	19 what
20 all	20 saw

Form A   Graded Word Lists

1	new		1	birthday
2	leg		2	free
3	feet		3	isn't
4	hear		4	beautiful
5	food		5	job
6	learn		6	elephant
7	hat		7	cowboy
8	ice		8	branch
9	letter		9	asleep
10	green		10	mice
11	outside		11	corn
12	happy		12	baseball
13	less		13	garden
14	drop		14	hall
15	stopping		15	pet
16	grass		16	blows
17	street		17	gray
18	page		18	law
19	ever		19	bat
20	let's		20	guess

Form A   Graded Word Lists

1	distant		1	unhappy
2	phone		2	jug
3	turkeys		3	innocent
4	crunch		4	relax
5	chief		5	bound
6	foolish		6	seventeen
7	engage		7	disturb
8	glow		8	glove
9	drain		9	compass
10	fully		10	attractive
11	crowd		11	impact
12	energy		12	lettuce
13	passenger		13	operator
14	shark		14	regulation
15	vacation		15	violet
16	pencil		16	settlers
17	goodness		17	merrily
18	discover		18	internal
19	polite		19	drama
20	nail		20	landscape

Form A   Graded Word Lists

1	moan	1	brisk
2	hymn	2	nostrils
3	bravely	3	marsh
4	dispose	4	headlight
5	shrill	5	calmly
6	jewel	6	farthest
7	loudly	7	wreath
8	register	8	emptiness
9	embarrass	9	billows
10	graceful	10	knight
11	cube	11	instinct
12	scarf	12	harpoon
13	muffled	13	pounce
14	pacing	14	rumor
15	oars	15	dazzle
16	biblical	16	combustion
17	thermometer	17	hearth
18	zone	18	mockingbird
19	salmon	19	ridiculous
20	magical	20	widen

F O R M   A

Part 2 Graded Paragraphs

Designed for Elementary School Children (grades 1–6)

The Play Car

"See my play car," said Tom.
"It can go fast."
Ann said, "It's a big car."
"Yes," said Tom.
"Would you like a ride?"

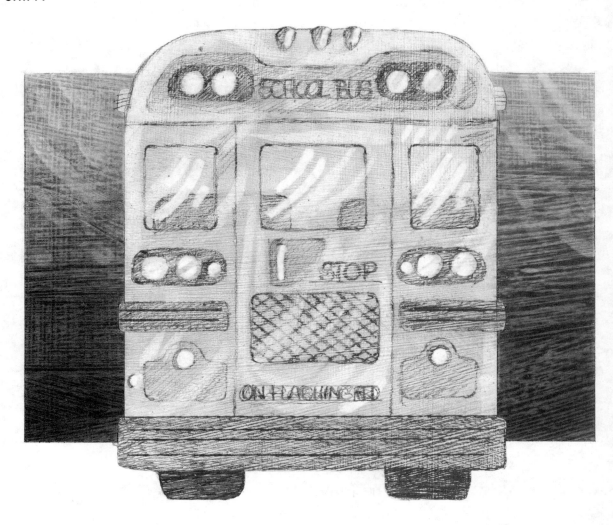

Our Bus Ride

It was time to go to the farm.
"Get in the bus," said Mrs. Brown.
"We are ready to go now."
The children climbed into the bus.
Away went the bus.
It was a good day for a ride.

Puppies

Puppies are fun to watch.
They are born with their eyes closed.
Their ears are closed, too.
This is why they use their touch and smell.
Puppies open their eyes and ears after two weeks.
By four weeks most puppies can bark.
Puppies grow up to make good pets.

A Simple Telephone

You can make your own private telephone.
You will need two empty tin cans and some string.
The two cans must have the tops cut off.
Punch a small hole in the bottom of each can.
Push the string through the holes and tie the string ends in a knot.
Give someone a can and ask them to move away.
The string must be straight and tight.
One of you should speak into the open end of the "telephone."
The other person will hear the voice as it moves along the string.
Now you have a "simple telephone."

Strange Facts about Elephants

Elephants are unusual animals. They take showers by shooting a stream of water from their trunks. An elephant uses its trunk to carry heavy logs. Elephants also use their trunks to breathe, smell, and eat.

A frightened elephant can run at a speed of more than 25 miles per hour. On a long journey an elephant travels at about 10 miles per hour. The gray skin of an elephant looks thick and strong. It's not—flies and other insects can bite into the skin.

When you go to the zoo, be sure to visit the elephants.

French Fried Tubers?

Tubers are another name for potatoes. Most potatoes are grown in Idaho, Maine, and New York. We like to bake, boil, mash, and French fry potatoes. We like French fries most of all.

Farmers must plant and pick their potatoes each year. Machines are used to dig up the potatoes from the soil. The potatoes are washed, peeled, and sliced. After they are fried in hot oil, they are frozen stiff and shipped to different places. Tons of French fries are prepared and sold each year.

How many times have you asked for a "hamburger and French fries?" Next time ask for French fried tubers.

Electric Cars

Will the cars of the future be electric cars? Many people hope so because electric cars might solve some of our pollution problems.

Electric cars have advantages and disadvantages.

Some advantages are: they do not produce exhaust fumes or use oil. They cost less and owners can recharge the batteries at home or at work.

Some disadvantages are: electric cars can travel only about 100 miles and then the batteries must be recharged. The batteries must be replaced over the lifetime of the car. Today's electric car can go only about 60 miles per hour.

Electric cars will not solve all of our problems, but they do seem to be our best hope for the future.

Blaze: Rebel Horse

All the ranchers in the valley knew about the wild stallion named Blaze, a powerful horse with a red mane. Many of the local men tried to catch this rebel but failed each time. A reward was offered for his capture—dead or alive, because he encouraged other horses to run away with him.

Pete Cook and six other men were determined to catch Blaze. Pete used binoculars to study the wild horse's movements. He made several maps of the valley and was sure he could capture Blaze this time.

Pete posted the men along the secluded trails that Blaze usually followed. Each rider would pick up Blaze along the trail and force him into a narrow canyon, where Pete would be waiting.

The men succeeded in forcing Blaze into the narrow canyon. Pete was ready with his rope, but Blaze came at him in a wild rage. Pete lost his balance but was able to roll over out of the way. Blaze saw his chance to escape and got away once again.

Salt Flat Speed

Rolling up to the starting line at Utah's Bonneville Salt Flats was a racing car that looked like something designed by Dr. Frankenstein on his day off. It had "Green Monster" emblazoned on its side. It was so ugly that some called it "the garbage truck." Over the huge jet intake on its nose was a short wing that looked like a coffee table. Bulging from its side was a cockpit in which the driver steered the car lying almost flat. But the Green Monster soon demonstrated that it was no truck.

Howling like a banshee, it streaked through the measured mile at 396 miles per hour. Then it turned around and sped back through the mile once more. This time the speed was 479 miles per hour. U.S. Auto Club officials checked their electronic timers and averaged the two runs. Art Arfons, the Green Monster's builder and driver, had set a new world's land-speed mark of 437.5 miles per hour! Racing cars now travel over 600 miles per hour.

Amazing Amelia

Amelia Earhart worked to open up new careers for women. She might easily qualify as an early feminist. When World War I ended, there were still a great many fields closed to women. Despite this, Amelia decided to go to medical school. In 1919 it was very difficult for women to get into medical school. Amelia persisted and did get into medical school. After her first year of school, Amelia decided to become a pilot.

After only ten hours of training, this amazing woman set a new world flying record. She flew to a height of over two miles.

Soon after this Amelia and an all male crew made a flight across the Atlantic Ocean. This record-breaking flight took exactly twenty hours and forty minutes.

Until her death in 1937, Amelia continued to challenge many things that were thought to be impossible.

FORM A

Inventory Record for Teachers

Summary Sheet

Student's Name _____ Grade _____ Age (Chronological) _____

yrs. mos.

Date _____ School _____ Administered by _____

Part 1 Word Lists			Part 2 Graded Paragraphs		
Grade Level	Percent of Words Correct	Word Recognition Errors		SIG WR	Comp	L.C.

Grade Level	Percent of Words Correct	Word Recognition Errors		SIG WR	Comp	L.C.
PP		**Consonants**	PP			
P (1)	_____	___ consonants	P			
1	_____	___ blends	1			
	_____	___ digraphs	2			
		___ endings	3			
		___ compounds				
		___ contractions	4			
		Vowels	5			
		___ long	6			
		___ short	7			
		___ long/short oo	8			
2	_____	___ vowel + r				
		___ diphthong				
		___ vowel comb.				
		___ a + 1 or w				
		Syllable				
3	_____	___ visual patterns				
4	_____	___ prefix				
		___ suffix				
5	_____	Word Recognition reinforcement and Vocabulary development				
6	_____					

Estimated Levels

Grade

Independent _____

Instructional _____ (range)

Frustration _____

Listening Capacity _____

Comp Errors

_____ Factual (F)

_____ Inference (I)

_____ Vocabulary (V)

_____ "Word Caller"
(A student who
reads without asso-
ciating meaning)

_____ Poor Memory

Summary of Specific Needs:

Permission is granted by the publisher to reproduce pp. 59 through 70.

Form A   Part 1   Graded Word Lists

PP		P		1		2	
1 this	_____	1 came	_____	1 new	_____	1 birthday	_____
2 her	_____	2 day	_____	2 leg	_____	2 free	_____
3 about	_____	3 up	_____	3 feet	_____	3 isn't	_____
4 to	_____	4 was	_____	4 hear	_____	4 beautiful	_____
5 and	_____	5 after	_____	5 food	_____	5 job	_____
6 it	_____	6 now	_____	6 learn	_____	6 elephant	_____
7 he	_____	7 read	_____	7 hat	_____	7 cowboy	_____
8 for	_____	8 other	_____	8 ice	_____	8 branch	_____
9 like	_____	9 went	_____	9 letter	_____	9 asleep	_____
10 can	_____	10 just	_____	10 green	_____	10 mice	_____
11 big	_____	11 play	_____	11 outside	_____	11 corn	_____
12 said	_____	12 many	_____	12 happy	_____	12 baseball	_____
13 house	_____	13 trees	_____	13 less	_____	13 garden	_____
14 look	_____	14 time	_____	14 drop	_____	14 hall	_____
15 go	_____	15 good	_____	15 stopping	_____	15 pet	_____
16 see	_____	16 into	_____	16 grass	_____	16 blows	_____
17 there	_____	17 we	_____	17 street	_____	17 gray	_____
18 little	_____	18 something	_____	18 page	_____	18 law	_____
19 is	_____	19 what	_____	19 ever	_____	19 bat	_____
20 all	_____	20 saw	_____	20 let's	_____	20 guess	_____
		_____%		_____%		_____%	_____%

Teacher note: If the child misses five words in any column, stop Part 1. Begin Graded Paragraphs, Part 2 (Form A), at the highest level in which the child recognized all 20 words. To save time, if the first ten words were correct, go on to the next list. If one of the words was missed, continue the entire list.

3		4		5		6	
1 distant	_____	1 unhappy	_____	1 moan	_____	1 brisk	_____
2 phone	_____	2 jug	_____	2 hymn	_____	2 nostrils	_____
3 turkeys	_____	3 innocent	_____	3 bravely	_____	3 marsh	_____
4 crunch	_____	4 relax	_____	4 dispose	_____	4 headlight	_____
5 chief	_____	5 bound	_____	5 shrill	_____	5 calmly	_____
6 foolish	_____	6 seventeen	_____	6 jewel	_____	6 farthest	_____
7 engage	_____	7 disturb	_____	7 loudly	_____	7 wreath	_____
8 glow	_____	8 glove	_____	8 register	_____	8 emptiness	_____
9 drain	_____	9 compass	_____	9 embarrass	_____	9 billows	_____
10 fully	_____	10 attractive	_____	10 graceful	_____	10 knight	_____
11 crowd	_____	11 impact	_____	11 cube	_____	11 instinct	_____
12 energy	_____	12 lettuce	_____	12 scarf	_____	12 harpoon	_____
13 passenger	_____	13 operator	_____	13 muffled	_____	13 pounce	_____
14 shark	_____	14 regulation	_____	14 pacing	_____	14 rumor	_____
15 vacation	_____	15 violet	_____	15 oars	_____	15 dazzle	_____
16 pencil	_____	16 settlers	_____	16 biblical	_____	16 combustion	_____
17 goodness	_____	17 merrily	_____	17 thermometer	_____	17 hearth	_____
18 discover	_____	18 internal	_____	18 zone	_____	18 mockingbird	_____
19 polite	_____	19 drama	_____	19 salmon	_____	19 ridiculous	_____
20 nail	_____	20 landscape	_____	20 magical	_____	20 widen	_____
	_____%		_____%		_____%		_____%

Form A   Part 2/Level PP (24 Words)

Background Knowledge Assessment:[15] This story is about two children and their play car. Tell what you think the children are doing.   adequate☐   inadequate☐

The Play Car

"See my play car," said Tom.

"It can go fast."

Ann said, "It's a big car."

"Yes," said Tom.

"Would you like a ride?"

Scoring Guide Preprimer

SIG WR Errors		COMP Errors	
IND	0	IND	0–1
INST	1–2	INST	1½–2
FRUST	3+	FRUST	2½+

Comprehension Check

(F) 1. _____ What are the names of the boy and girl in the story?
(Tom and Ann)

(F) 2. _____ What were they talking about?
(The play car, etc.)

(F) 3. _____ Who owned the car?
(Tom)

(F) 4. _____ What did Ann (the girl) say about the car?
(Big car)

(I) 5. _____ What do you think Tom might have liked about the car.
(It was fast, big.)

Form A   Part 2/Level P (39 words)

Background Knowledge Assessment: Has your class even taken a field trip? What can you tell about field trips?   adequate☐   inadequate☐

Our Bus Ride

It was time to go to the farm.

"Get in the bus," said Mrs. Brown.

"We are ready to go now."

The children climbed into the bus.

Away went the bus.

It was a good day for a ride.

Scoring Guide Primer

SIG WR Errors		COMP Errors	
IND	0	IND	0–1
INST	2	INST	1½–2
FRUST	4+	FRUST	2½+

Comprehension Check

(F) 1. _____ Where were they going?
(Farm)

(F) 2. _____ How were they going?
(By bus)

(I) 3. _____ Who do you think Mrs. Brown was?
(Teacher, or bus driver)

(F) 4. _____ How did the children know that it was time for the bus to leave?
(Mrs. Brown said, "We are ready to go now.")

(F) 5. _____ Was this bus ride taking place during the day or at night?
(Day)

---

15. See page 5 for a discussion of Background Knowledge Assessment.

Form A   Part 2/Level 1 (49 Words)

Background Knowledge Assessment: This story is about puppies. What can you tell me about puppies?

adequate ☐   inadequate ☐

Puppies

Puppies are fun to watch.

They are born with their eyes closed.

Their ears are closed, too.

This is why they use their touch and smell.

Puppies open their eyes and ears after two weeks.

By four weeks most puppies can bark.

Puppies grow up to make good pets.

Scoring Guide   First

SIG WR Errors		COMP Errors	
IND	0	IND	0–1
INST	2	INST	1½–2
FRUST	4+	FRUST	2½+

Comprehension Check

(F) 1. ____ When puppies are born, are their eyes open or closed?
(closed)

(F) 2. ____ At birth puppies must use their touch and smell. Why?
(eyes closed or ears closed)

(F) 3. ____ How long does it take for puppies to open their eyes and ears?
(2 weeks)

(F) 4. ____ What can puppies do after 4 weeks?
(Bark)

(I) 5. ____ Why do you think puppies are fun to watch?
(they jump, run around, roll around)

Form A   Part 2/Level 2 (98 Words)

Background Knowledge Assessment: This story tells how to make a simple telephone. How often do you use the telephone?   adequate☐   inadequate☐

A Simple Telephone

You can make your own private telephone. You will need two empty tin cans and some string. The two cans must have the tops cut off. Punch a small hole in the bottom of each can. Push the string through the holes and tie the string ends in a knot. Give someone a can and ask them to move away. The string must be straight and tight. One of you should speak into the open end of the "telephone." The other person will hear the voice as it moves along the string. Now you have a "simple telephone."

Comprehension Check

(F)   1. ____ Name two things you need to make a simple telephone.
(cans and string)

(F)   2. ____ What do you need to do to the cans?
(cut tops off and/or punch a hole in bottoms)

(I)   3. ____ Why do you have to tie knots in the string?
(so string won't slip out of can)

(I)   4. ____ Why should the string be straight and tight?
(so voice can move along string)

(I)   5. ____ Why do you think two people must be far away from each other when they talk on the "phone?"
(they can hear each other without the phone)

Scoring Guide   Second

SIG WR Errors		COMP Errors	
IND	2	IND	0–1
INST	5	INST	1½–2
FRUST	10	FRUST	2½+

Background Knowledge Assessment: What can you tell me about elephants?

adequate ☐   inadequate ☐

Strange Facts About Elephants

Elephants are unusual animals. They take showers by shooting a stream of water from their trunks. An elephant uses its trunk to carry heavy logs. Elephants also use their trunks to breathe, smell, and eat.

A frightened elephant can run at a speed of more than 25 miles per hour. On a long journey an elephant travels at about 10 miles per hour. The gray skin of an elephant looks thick and strong. It's not—flies and other insects can bite into the skin.

When you go to the zoo, be sure to visit the elephants.

Scoring Guide   Third

SIG WR Errors		COMP Errors	
IND	2	IND	0–1
INST	5	INST	1½–2
FRUST	10	FRUST	2½+

Comprehension Check

(F)   1. ____ Tell two of the ways elephants use their trunks.
(shoot water, breathe, smell, eat, carry logs)

(F)   2. ____ If frightened an elephant can run at what speed?
(25 m.p.h.)

(I)   3. ____ The skin of an elephant is not as strong as it looks. Why do you think this is?
(flies and insects can bite into the skin)

(F)   4. ____ How fast do elephants travel on long trips?
(10 m.p.h.)

(V)   5. ____ What does the word journey mean?
(a long trip, travel)

Background Knowledge Assessment: Do you like to eat potatoes? How do you like them cooked? Tell me more.   adequate☐   inadequate☐

French Fried Tubers?

Tubers are another name for potatoes. Most potatoes are grown in Idaho, Maine, and New York. We like to bake, boil, mash, and French fry potatoes. We like French fries most of all.

Farmers must plant and pick their potatoes each year. Machines are used to dig up the potatoes from the soil. The potatoes are washed, peeled, and sliced. After they are fried in hot oil, they are frozen stiff and shipped to different places. Tons of French fries are prepared and sold each year.

How many times have you asked for a "hamburger and French fries?" Next time ask for French fried tubers.

Comprehension Check

(F) 1. ＿＿＿ What is another name for potatoes? (tubers)

(F) 2. ＿＿＿ What kind of potatoes do most people like to eat? (French fried potatoes)

(I) 3. ＿＿＿ Do potatoes grow above or below the ground? (below)

(V) 4. ＿＿＿ What does prepared mean? (make ready, put in condition for something)

(F) 5. ＿＿＿ Name one of the states where most potatoes are grown. (Idaho, Maine, or New York)

Scoring Guide Fourth

SIG WR Errors		COMP Errors	
IND	2	IND	0–1
INST	6	INST	1½–2
FRUST	11	FRUST	2½+

Form A   Part 2/Level 5 (115 Words)

Background Knowledge Assessment: What can you tell me about electric cars?

adequate☐   inadequate☐

Electric Cars

Will the cars of the future be electric cars? Many people hope so because electric cars might solve some of our pollution problems.

Electric cars have advantages and disadvantages.

Some advantages are: they do not produce exhaust fumes or use oil. They cost less and owners can recharge the batteries at home or at work.

Some disadvantages are: electric cars can travel only about 100 miles and then the batteries must be recharged. The batteries must be replaced over the lifetime of the car. Today's electric car can go only about 60 miles per hour.

Electric cars will not solve all of our problems, but they do seem to be our best hope for the future.

Comprehension Check

(V) 1. _____ What word was used that means unclean air or fuel exhaust? (pollution)

(F) 2. _____ Give me some advantages for using electric cars. (no exhaust, do not use oil, costs less, batteries easily charged)

(F) 3. _____ Give me some disadvantages. (can only travel 100 miles, batteries need to be replaced, top speed 60 m.p.h.)

(I) 4. _____ How would electric cars reduce or solve some of our problems? (reduce pollution, less need for oil)

(I) 5. _____ What might happen if we continue to pollute the environment? (poor health, run out of oil, we might die)

Scoring Guide   Fifth

SIG WR Errors		COMP Errors	
IND	2	IND	0–1
INST	6	INST	1½–2
FRUST	11	FRUST	2½+

Form A   Part 2/Level 6 (174 Words)

Background Knowledge Assessment: This story tells about how a group of men attempted to capture a wild horse. What are some things these men would have to do to capture this wild horse?

adequate☐   inadequate☐

Blaze: Rebel Horse

All the ranchers in the valley knew about the wild stallion named Blaze, a powerful horse with a red mane. Many of the local men tried to catch this rebel but failed each time. A reward was offered for his capture—dead or alive, because he encouraged other horses to run away with him.

Pete Cook and six other men were determined to catch Blaze. Pete used binoculars to study the wild horse's movements. He made several maps of the valley and was sure he could capture Blaze this time.

Pete posted the men all along the secluded trails that Blaze usually followed. Each rider would pick up Blaze along the trail and force him into a narrow canyon, where Pete would be waiting.

The men succeeded in forcing Blaze into the narrow canyon. Pete was ready with his rope, but Blaze came at him in a wild rage. Pete lost his balance but was able to roll over out of the way. Blaze saw his chance to escape and got away once again.

Comprehension Check

(F) 1. ____ Why did the ranchers want the wild horse (Blaze) captured?
(He encouraged other horses to run away.)

(F) 2. ____ What did the wild horse (Blaze) look like?
(Powerful, big, red mane)

(F) 3. ____ What did Pete Cook do before attempting to capture Blaze?
(He made maps of the valley and of the horse's trails.)

(V) 4. ____ What does "secluded" mean?
(Hidden, secret, hard to find)

(I) 5. ____ Describe how you think Pete's men worked to capture Blaze.
(They spread out and forced him into a narrow canyon, they teamed up)

Scoring Guide   Sixth

SIG WR Errors		COMP Errors	
IND	3	IND	0–1
INST	8	INST	1½–2
FRUST	17	FRUST	2½+

Form A   Part 2/Level 7 (166 words)

Background Knowledge Assessment: Fast cars are interesting to some people. Highways are designed to allow cars to travel at 55 miles per hour. Imagine a car that traveled faster than 600 mph.

adequate ☐   inadequate ☐

Salt Flat Speed

Rolling up to the starting line at Utah's Bonneville Salt Flats was a racing car that looked like something designed by Dr. Frankenstein on his day off. It had "Green Monster" emblazoned on its side. It was so ugly that some called it "the garbage truck." Over the huge jet intake on its nose was a short wing that looked like a coffee table. Bulging from its side was a cockpit in which the driver steered the car lying almost flat. But the Green Monster soon demonstated that it was no truck.

Howling like a banshee, it streaked through the measured mile at 396 miles per hour. Then it turned around and sped back through the mile once more. This time the speed was 479 miles per hour. U.S. Auto Club officials checked their electronic timers and averaged the two runs. Art Arfrons, the Green Monster's builder and driver, had set a new world's land-speed mark of 437.5 miles per hour! Racing cars now travel over 600 miles per hour.

Comprehension Check

(F) 1. _____ What was the name of this car?
(Green Monster)

(F) 2. _____ Why did some people call this car a "garbage truck"?
(Because it was ugly, because they didn't think it could set a record)

(F) 3. _____ What did the race car have over its jet intake on the nose of the car?
(A short wing)

(V) 4. _____ The words "howled like a banshee" were used in this selection. What does that mean?
(A wailing, screeching, eerie noise)

(I) 5. _____ Why won't we see the Green Monster or a car like it driving along our streets?
(Car is too fast)

Scoring Guide   Seventh

SIG WR Errors		COMP Errors	
IND	3	IND	0–1
INST	7–8	INST	1½–2
FRUST	15	FRUST	2½+

Background Knowledge Assessment: Amelia Earhart was a courageous pioneer. Read these paragraphs to learn more about this courageous woman.   adequate ☐   inadequate ☐

Amazing Amelia

Amelia Earhart worked to open up new careers for women. She might easily qualify as an early feminist. When World War I ended, there were still a great many fields closed to women. Despite this, Amelia decided to go to medical school. In 1919 it was very difficult for women to get into medical school. Amelia persisted and did get into medical school. After her first year of school, Amelia decided to become a pilot.

After only ten hours of training, this amazing woman set a new world flying record. She flew to a height of over two miles.

Soon after this, Amelia and an all male crew made a flight across the Atlantic Ocean. This record-breaking flight took exactly twenty hours and forty minutes.

Until her death in 1937, Amelia continued to challenge many things that were thought to be impossible.

Comprehension Check

(F) 1. ____ Why did Amelia leave medical college?
(To become a pilot, didn't like medical college)

(V) 2. ____ What does "feminist" mean?
(A person who is attempting to provide equal opportunities for women)

(F) 3. ____ How high did Amelia fly when she set a new world record?
(Over two miles)

(V) 4. ____ The word persisted was used. What does "persisted" mean?
(Refused to give up, to endure, etc.)

(I) 5. ____ What do you think is meant by this statement: "Amelia challenged the impossible"?
(She tried to break the world flying records. She wanted new opportunities for women, etc.)

Scoring Guide   Eighth

SIG WR Errors		COMP Errors	
IND	3	IND	0–1
INST	7	INST	1½–2
FRUST	14	FRUST	2½+

F O R M   B

Literature Based Selections

Designed for Elementary School Children (grades 1–6)

It's My Ball

Tom and Nancy went for a walk.
They saw a small ball on the grass.
They began fighting over the ball.
While they were fighting, a dog picked up the ball and ran.
The kids ran after the dog, but the dog got away.

Fish for Sale

Susan got ten fish and a tank for her birthday.

She loved the fish and learned to take good care of them.

One day Susan saw six new baby fish in the tank.

The fish tank was too small for all of the fish.

Dad said he would buy another tank for the baby fish.

Everyone began giving Susan fish and equipment.

Soon she had tanks for big fish, small fish, and baby fish.

Each tank had water plants, air tubes, and stones on the bottom.

Mom said, "Enough! Susan, your room looks like a store for fish."

That gave Susan an idea. Why not put all of the fish tanks in the garage and put up a sign?

Susan and her Dad moved everything into the garage.

Susan made a big sign that read "FISH FOR SALE."

The Fox—A Farmer's Friend

"Meg, look! That's a female fox ready to have cubs." Uncle Mike was excited, "I haven't seen a fox around here for ten years." Meg said, "Shall I get your gun?" "There's no need for a gun," Uncle Mike replied. "Foxes help farmers by eating pests like mice, squirrels, frogs, and insects."

The next day Meg and her uncle were unhappy to learn that some farmers were hunting for the fox. These farmers didn't believe that a fox was helpful. Foxes save the farmers' crops by eating pests that destroy their crops. The farmers were sure that foxes only killed chickens and other small animals.

After weeks of hunting, the farmers gave up trying to kill the fox. When Uncle Mike and Meg found fresh fox and cub tracks, on the far end of their farm, they were happy.

Floods Are Dangerous

Mrs. Foley was driving home with her two sons, nine-year-old Peter and eleven-year-old Jason. Lightning flashed, thunder shook the ground, and the rain poured down. In order to get home, Mrs. Foley had to cross a road covered with water. She decided to drive across the rushing water. When the car was about halfway, the water rose higher, and the car began to float away. Mrs. Foley knew that she had to get the boys and herself out of that car.

Eleven-year-old Jason was able to roll down the window and jump to a small hill. Mrs. Foley also jumped to the hill. Mrs. Foley and Jason tried to grab Peter, but the car was pushed downstream.

Soon the police and friends came, and they searched all night for Peter. Peter was nowhere to be seen. Had Peter drowned in the flood, or was he safe?

Early the next day Mrs. Foley heard horns blowing and neighbors shouting, "Peter is safe." Peter told everyone how he got out of the car but then he got lost in the dark. Everyone was happy to see Peter again.

The Great Railroad

President Lincoln had a dream for the future. He wanted a railroad built between Nebraska and California. In 1862, Mr. Lincoln's dream began to come true when he signed the Pacific Railroad Act. Soon after, he employed Mr. Dodge, an engineer, to direct the building of the railroad.

Mr. Dodge decided to build the railroad in two directions. He used one company called the Central Pacific Railroad to work from California eastward. The other was called the Union Pacific Railroad. They worked from Nebraska westward. More than 20,000 workers, many of whom were Chinese, were soon laying track from east and west.

In this project, costs were high and problems were many. Each company had to transport such things as food, clothing, medicine, and track. The workers had to blast tunnels, build bridges, and cross high, snow-covered mountains.

On May 10, 1869, leaders of both companies drove a golden spike into the final rail. Mr. Dodge, the project director, had tears in his eyes as the two trains touched. He thought about his first meeting with Lincoln. Mr. Dodge was happy that the railroad was completed but sad that President Lincoln did not live to see his dream come true.

A Different Kind of Courage

Mike overheard an older guy named Buster bragging about the fact that he skied the old abandoned ski trail called **Killer Hill.** Mike, a sixth grader, decided that if Buster could do it so could he. Mike told his parents that he wanted to ski **Killer Hill.**

"You gone off your head Mike?" his father said. "That darn trail could kill you."

Mike knew the risks, and he feared them. While getting ready for bed, he thought maybe he was a fool, but he wouldn't stop now.

While Mike, his parents, and his two best friends were driving to the ski slopes, his father said, "Why do you want to do such a crazy thing?"

Mike thought, how could he explain that he wanted to show up Buster.

Mike's father was saying, "That hill is dangerous. Use the regular trails."

Mike whispered, "Regular trails are for kids."

His father grinned, "Maybe so—but be careful son."

"I will, Pop, I promise."

When they reached the top of the ski lift, Mike headed for **Killer Hill.** He didn't realize it, but his friends and others, including Buster, followed him. Mike was about to push off when his friends yelled, "Mike—don't do it!" This caused him to hesitate.

Buster shouted, "What's the matter—are you chicken?"

Mike's friends were excited and screamed, "Mike, please, please don't do it."

Suddenly he knew they were right; he was trying to show off—just like Buster. Mike turned and joined his friends.

He wished he could tell how it was—that it was harder to let Buster think he was yellow than it would have been to ski the trail.

Mike couldn't explain it, but it took a different kind of courage to let himself be ridiculed for something others couldn't understand.

FORM B

Inventory Record for Teachers

FORM B Inventory Record _____

Summary Sheet

Student's Name _____ Grade _____ Age _____
(yr) (mo)

Prediction–Retelling					
Level	Prediction	Character(s)	Problem	Outcome	Total
1					
2					
3					
4					
5					
6					

Prompting		
Very Little	Ave	Needs Help

Comfortable Reading Level		
Above	Ave	Below

Summary of Specific Instructional Needs:

Ability to Predict: _____

Ability to Retell: _____

_____

Prompting to obtain predicting and retelling responses: _____

_____

Comments: _____

_____

Comfortable Reading Level: _____

Notes, Comments, and Observations

Teacher Record Sheet

Use this teacher record sheet for notes, comments, and observations of students' reactions to the literature-based form.

_____

_____

_____

_____

_____

_____

_____

_____

_____

_____

_____

_____

_____

_____

_____

_____

_____

Form B, Level 1

It's My Ball

Tom and Nancy went for a walk.

They saw a small ball on the grass.

They began fighting over the ball.

While they were fighting, a dog picked

up the ball and ran.

The kids ran after the dog, but the

dog got away.

Comfortable Reading Level
-fluent (above _____ ave _____ below _____)

	Low			High	(circle number)
	1	2	3	4	5

PREDICTION: **Picture and Title**
What do you think the story will be about?

_____

_____

_____

Retelling:
CHARACTERS   1   2   3   4   5
What do you remember about the people in the story?

_____

_____

_____

Problem   1   2   3   4   5
What was the problem? If you were in that situation
   what would you do?

_____

_____

_____

Outcome   1   2   3   4   5
How was the problem solved?

_____

_____

TOTAL SCORE _____

SCORING GUIDE:
16 to 20
6 to 15
5 or less

First
Comprehension excellent
Needs assistance
Too difficult

Prompting:
very little _____
average _____
needs help _____

Form B, Level 2

Fish for Sale

Susan got ten fish and a tank for her birthday.

She loved the fish and learned to take good care of

them.

One day Susan saw six new baby fish in the tank.

The fish tank was too small for all of the fish.

Dad said he would buy another tank for the baby

fish.

Everyone began giving Susan fish and equipment.

Soon she had tanks for big fish, small fish, and baby

fish.

Each tank had water plants, air tubes, and stones

on the bottom.

Mom said, "Enough! Susan, your room looks like a

store for fish."

That gave Susan an idea. Why not put all of the

fish tanks in the garage and put up a sign?

Susan and her Dad moved everything into the

garage.

Susan made a big sign that read, "FISH FOR

SALE."

Student Responses

Low   High   (circle number)

1   2   3   4   5

PREDICTION: Picture and Title
What do you think is meant by the title, "Fish for
Sale?" What do you think the story will be about?

_____

_____

_____

Retelling:
CHARACTERS   1   2   3   4   5
What do you remember about the people in the story?

_____

_____

_____

Problem   1   2   3   4   5
What was the problem? What would you do if you had
this problem?

_____

_____

_____

Outcome   1   2   3   4   5
How was the problem solved? What do you think
Susan's goal was?

_____

_____

_____

Form B, Level 3

The Fox—A Farmer's Friend

"Meg, look! That's a female fox ready to have cubs."
Uncle Mike was excited, "I haven't seen a fox around
here for ten years." Meg said, "Shall I get your gun?"
"There's no need for a gun," Uncle Mike replied.
"Foxes help farmers by eating pests like mice, squir-
rels, frogs, and insects."

The next day Meg and her uncle were unhappy
to learn that some farmers were hunting for the fox.
These farmers didn't believe that a fox was helpful.
Foxes save the farmers' crops by eating pests that destroy their crops. The farmers were sure that foxes
only killed chickens and other small animals.

After weeks of hunting, the farmers gave up
trying to kill the fox. When Uncle Mike and Meg
found fresh fox and cub tracks, on the far end of their
farm, they were happy.

```
┌─────────────────────────────────────────────┐
│        Comfortable Reading Level              │
│  -fluent (above _____ ave _____ below _____ ) │
└─────────────────────────────────────────────┘
```

Student Responses

Low			High	(circle number)
1	2	3	4	5

PREDICTION: **Picture and Title**
Have you ever seen a fox? If no, discuss things about a
  fox? What do you think the story will be about?

_____

_____

_____

Retelling:
CHARACTERS   1   2   3   4   5
What can you tell me about the people in the story?

_____

_____

_____

Problem   1   2   3   4   5
The fox had a problem. What do you think was
  happening? Why do you think Meg and Uncle Mike
  worried?

_____

_____

_____

Outcome   1   2   3   4   5
What happened to the fox? When Uncle Mike and Meg
  saw the tracks, what did they learn? How did Uncle
  Mike and Meg feel?

_____

_____

_____

TOTAL SCORE _____

SCORING GUIDE:
16 to 20
6 to 15
5 or less

Third
Comprehension excellent
Needs assistance
Too difficult

Prompting:
very little _____
average _____
needs help _____

Form B, Level 4

Floods Are Dangerous

Mrs. Foley was driving home with her two sons, nine-year-old Peter and eleven-year-old Jason. Lightning flashed, thunder shook the ground, and the rain poured down. In order to get home, Mrs. Foley had to cross a road covered with water. She decided to drive across the rushing water. When the car was about halfway, the water rose higher, and the car began to float away. Mrs. Foley knew that she had to get the boys and herself out of that car.

Eleven-year-old Jason was able to roll down the window and jump to a small hill. Mrs. Foley also jumped to the hill. Mrs. Foley and Jason tried to grab Peter, but the car was pushed downstream.

Soon the police and friends came, and they searched all night for Peter. Peter was nowhere to be seen. Had Peter drowned in the flood, or was he safe?

Early the next day Mrs. Foley heard horns blowing and neighbors shouting, "Peter is safe." Peter told everyone how he got out of the car but then he got lost in the dark. Everyone was happy to see Peter again.

> **Comfortable Reading Level**
> -fluent (above _____ ave _____ below _____)

Student Responses

	Low			High	(circle number)
	1	2	3	4	5

PREDICTION: Picture and Title
What do you think the story will be about?

_____

_____

_____

Retelling:
CHARACTERS   1   2   3   4   5
What do you remember about the people in the story? How do you think they felt?

_____

_____

_____

Problem   1   2   3   4   5
What was the problem? What do you think caused the problem?

_____

_____

_____

Outcome   1   2   3   4   5
How do you think the problem was solved? How do you think you would feel in this situation?

_____

_____

_____

TOTAL SCORE _____

SCORING GUIDE:	Fourth	Prompting:
16 to 20	Comprehension excellent	very little _____
6 to 15	Needs assistance	average _____
5 or less	Too difficult	needs help _____

Form B, Level 5

The Great Railroad

President Lincoln had a dream for the future. He wanted a railroad built between Nebraska and California. In 1862, Mr. Lincoln's dream began to come true when he signed the Pacific Railroad Act. Soon after, he employed Mr. Dodge, an engineer, to direct the building of the railroad.

Mr. Dodge decided to build the railroad in two directions. He used one company called the Central Pacific Railroad to work from California eastward. The other was called the Union Pacific Railroad. They worked from Nebraska westward. More than 20,000 workers, many of whom were Chinese, were soon laying track from east and west.

In this project, costs were high and problems were many. Each company had to transport such things as food, clothing, medicine, and track. The workers had to blast tunnels, build bridges, and cross high, snow-covered mountains.

On May 10, 1869, leaders of both companies drove a golden spike into the final rail. Mr. Dodge, the project director, had tears in his eyes as the two trains touched. He thought about his first meeting with Lincoln. Mr. Dodge was happy that the railroad was completed but sad that President Lincoln did not live to see his dream come true.

PREDICTION: **Picture and Title**
What do you remember about the story?

_____

_____

_____

Retelling:
CHARACTERS   1   2   3   4   5
In your opinion who was the main person or persons in the story?

_____

_____

_____

Problem   1   2   3   4   5
Why do you think Mr. Dodge used two companies?
What types of problems did these companies have?

_____

_____

_____

Outcome   1   2   3   4   5
What in your opinion was the goal?

_____

_____

_____

Comfortable Reading Level
-fluent (above _____ ave _____ below _____)

TOTAL SCORE _____

SCORING GUIDE:
16 to 20
6 to 15
5 or less

Fifth
Comprehension excellent
Needs assistance
Too difficult

Prompting:
very little _____
average _____
needs help _____

Form B, Level 6

A Different Kind of Courage

Mike overheard an older guy named Buster bragging about the fact that he skied the old abandoned ski trail called **Killer Hill.** Mike, a sixth grader, decided that if Buster could do it so could he. Mike told his parents that he wanted to ski **Killer Hill.**

"You gone off your head Mike?" his father said. "That darn trail could kill you."

Mike knew the risks, and he feared them. While getting ready for bed, he thought maybe he was a fool, but he wouldn't stop now.

While Mike, his parents, and his two best friends were driving to the ski slopes, his father said, "Why do you want to do such a crazy thing?" Mike thought, how could he explain that he wanted to show up Buster. Mike's father was saying, "That hill is dangerous. Use the regular trails." Mike whispered, "Regular trails are for kids." His father grinned, "Maybe so—but be careful son."

"I will, Pop, I promise."

When they reached the top of the ski lift, Mike headed for **Killer Hill.** He didn't realize it, but his friends and others, including Buster, followed him. Mike was about to push off when his friends yelled, "Mike—don't do it!" This caused him to hesitate.

Buster shouted, "What's the matter—are you chicken?" Mike's friends were excited and screamed, "Mike, please, please don't do it." Suddenly he knew they were right; he was trying to show off—just like Buster. Mike turned and joined his friends. He wished he could tell how it was—that it was harder to let Buster think he was yellow than it would have been to ski the trail.

Mike couldn't explain it, but it took a different kind of courage to let himself be ridiculed for something others couldn't understand.

FORM C

Part 1 Graded Word Lists

Designed for Junior High School Students

Form C

1 men	1 slide
2 nailed	2 clang
3 found	3 I'll
4 then	4 beauty
5 four	5 wheels
6 told	6 hand
7 him	7 chipmunk
8 place	8 right
9 night	9 pencil
10 another	10 twice
11 freight	11 torn
12 clock	12 together
13 garbage	13 strange
14 dress	14 dollars
15 grow	15 boats
16 frog	16 blow
17 struck	17 great
18 birthday	18 there's
19 peanut	19 mouth
20 don't	20 mail

Form C

1 soup	1 barrel
2 breath	2 awkward
3 remember	3 trial
4 afternoon	4 nephew
5 chief	5 fought
6 choose	6 experience
7 enough	7 dispose
8 enemy	8 cowards
9 cheese	9 wheat
10 dessert	10 trousers
11 inventor	11 mounted
12 cousin	12 iron
13 unusual	13 legends
14 clothing	14 ghost
15 drown	15 groan
16 plate	16 servants
17 scent	17 pitcher
18 disappointed	18 perched
19 posture	19 weight
20 pale	20 knowledge

Form C

1 whether

2 notched

3 sandals

4 pronged

5 sprinkle

6 shrill

7 length

8 contest

9 muscle

10 chant

11 excused

12 vinegar

13 shuffled

14 pierce

15 bore

16 delicious

17 orchard

18 territory

19 pouches

20 plateau

1 moisture

2 dorsal

3 contrary

4 sausage

5 notions

6 pounce

7 envelope

8 request

9 wreath

10 knights

11 irregular

12 torrent

13 salad

14 applause

15 hustling

16 tenor

17 hearth

18 surf

19 condition

20 official

Form C

1 numberless	1 pulverize
2 derby	2 custody
3 omen	3 delusion
4 rayon	4 barbarian
5 accumulate	5 privacy
6 dense	6 embankment
7 potential	7 designate
8 terrain	8 notorious
9 vivid	9 arrogant
10 segment	10 quote
11 amber	11 variation
12 humidity	12 pneumonia
13 monarch	13 embassy
14 publication	14 yacht
15 meteorite	15 authentic
16 ridicule	16 brigade
17 domestic	17 browse
18 focus	18 recruit
19 irregular	19 motive
20 algebra	20 belligerent

F O R M C

Part 2 Graded Paragraphs

Designed for Junior High School Students

Grasshoppers

Grasshoppers come from eggs. They have four long wings and six legs. Some grasshoppers live on the ground; others live in trees. All grasshoppers can jump and fly. They fly high in the air. They jump, fly, and play. Most grasshoppers are green, black, or brown.

The John F. Kennedy Space Center

A ball of fire is seen in the sky. The sky turns red and orange. Another rocket has been tested! Most rocket tests are made in Florida. The first test was made in 1958. In 1969 men were sent to the moon. People near the space center see rockets going off all the time. Almost every day is like the Fourth of July. We do not shoot them just for fun. We hope to learn things about space.

Yellowstone National Park

Each year more than two million people visit Yellowstone National Park. It is the largest of our national parks. The park is more than 8,000 feet above sea level. It has many natural hot water fountains called geysers. "Old Faithful" is the best-known of the geysers. It is not the largest, but is famous because it is so regular in its activity. "Old Faithful" shoots water and steam over 120 feet in the air. It does this about every 73 minutes, summer and winter. It has been doing this since early times! You can see why so many people visit this great park.

A Great American Sport

The history of baseball shows that the game has changed a great deal since it was first played. In 1839, Abner Doubleday set up the rules for playing a baseball game.

Later on, uniforms appeared. The players wore long pants, a fancy white shirt, and a straw hat. The umpire wore a long coat, a tall silk hat, and carried a cane. Rakes, ax handles, and tree branches were used as bats.

The first World Series was played in 1903. Baseball fans wanted to see the top teams from the two major leagues play. The winners would be the champions of the baseball world.

Driver Education

Even our parents may have some bad driving habits. This is why young drivers should take lessons from trained teachers.

A recent story makes this point. A young driver had learned from an older one. While driving, a young driver felt his two right wheels go off the road. He yanked the car quickly back onto the road. As a result, the car turned over. A passenger in the car was killed. A trained teacher would have taught the driver not to slam on the brakes. And not to turn back onto the road too quickly.

One of the best ways to decrease traffic accidents is to have more driver education.

Sentinels in the Forest

Many wild creatures that travel with their own kind know by instinct how to protect the group. One of them acts as a sentinel.

Hidden by the branches of a low-hanging tree, I once watched two white-tailed deer feeding in a meadow. At first, my interest was held by their beauty. But soon I noticed something which was quite unusual; they were taking turns at feeding.

One deer was calmly cropping grass, unafraid and at ease. The other, a sentinel, stood guard against enemies. The guard deer watched every movement and used its sensitive nostrils to "feel" the air. Not for a moment, during the half hour I spied upon them, did they stop their teamwork.

Modern Airports

In the earliest days of aviation, there was no need for airports. The light wood-and-cloth airplanes could take off and land in any level, open field.

In contrast to these simple airfields, the modern airport is almost a city in itself. There are many buildings and services for the convenience and comfort of the passengers.

Waiting rooms, restaurants, barbershops, post offices, banks, souvenir shops, florists, and even bowling alleys are likely to be located in the airport.

But the heart of the airport is still the area where the planes take off and land—the runways. Jet planes require very long runways—sometimes as much as two miles in length. Runways are paved with concrete to withstand the impact of planes weighing over 375 tons hitting the ground at speeds between 110 and 140 miles per hour. Taxiways link the runways with each other and with terminal buildings.

Sports Cars

To most laymen, a sports car is simply a vehicle with a flashy, streamlined body decorated with plenty of chrome. Such a vehicle, however, might easily be everything that an actual sports car should not be. It is the engineering features that the untrained eye does not observe which distinguish the true sports car from the bloated, over-chromed and highly colored dream cars that cruise along the American freeways on weekend afternoons.

The meticulously engineered features of a genuine sports car are those observed on the road rather than those idolized in the parking lots of country clubs. That which ordinarily is referred to as an American sports car would not be permitted to enter a European road race, because it would be too unsafe both for its own operator and for the other participants in a race. For another thing, it would be ridiculously outclassed for acceleration and roadability under conditions of such competitive driving.

F O R M   C

Inventory Record for Teachers

Designed for Junior High School Students

Form C may be used in any of the following ways.
1. As a set of *silent paragraphs* for students who
   might reject oral reading
2. As a set of *silent paragraphs* used with Form D
3. As a set of *paragraphs* for assessing the
   student's listening capacity level. (see p. 8)

Form C Inventory Record ━━━━━━━━━━━━━━━━━━━━

Summary Sheet

Student's Name _____ Grade _____ Age (Chronological) _____

yrs. mos.

Date _____ School _____ Administered by _____

Part 1 Word Lists			Part 2 Graded Paragraphs			
Grade Level	Percent of Words Correct	Word Recognition Errors		SIG WR	Comp	L.C.
1	———	**Consonants**	PP			
		—— consonants	P			
		—— blends	1			
		—— digraphs	2			
		—— endings	3			
		—— compounds	4			
2	———	—— contractions	5			
		Vowels	6			
		—— long	7			
		—— short	8			
		—— long / short oo				
		—— vowel + r	**Estimated Levels**			
		—— diphthong				
		—— vowel comb.		Grade		
		—— a + 1 or w	Independent	———		
		Syllable	Instructional	——— (range)		
3	———	—— visual patterns	Frustration	———		
4	———	—— prefix	Listening Capacity	———		
5	———	—— suffix				
6	———	**Word Recognition reinforcement and Vocabulary development**				
7	———					
8	———					

Comp Errors

——— Factual (F)

——— Inference (I)

——— Vocabulary (V)

——— "Word Caller"
   (A student who
   reads without asso-
   ciating meaning)

——— Poor Memory

Summary of Specific Needs:

Permission is granted by the publisher to reproduce pp. 107 through 117.

Form C Part 1 / Graded Word Lists

1		2		3		4	
1 men	_____	1 slide	_____	1 soup	_____	1 barrel	_____
2 nailed	_____	2 clang	_____	2 breath	_____	2 awkward	_____
3 found	_____	3 I'll	_____	3 remember	_____	3 trial	_____
4 then	_____	4 beauty	_____	4 afternoon	_____	4 nephew	_____
5 four	_____	5 wheels	_____	5 chief	_____	5 fought	_____
6 told	_____	6 hand	_____	6 choose	_____	6 experience	_____
7 him	_____	7 chipmunk	_____	7 enough	_____	7 dispose	_____
8 place	_____	8 right	_____	8 enemy	_____	8 cowards	_____
9 night	_____	9 pencil	_____	9 cheese	_____	9 wheat	_____
10 another	_____	10 twice	_____	10 dessert	_____	10 trousers	_____
11 freight	_____	11 torn	_____	11 inventor	_____	11 mounted	_____
12 clock	_____	12 together	_____	12 cousin	_____	12 iron	_____
13 garbage	_____	13 strange	_____	13 unusual	_____	13 legends	_____
14 dress	_____	14 dollars	_____	14 clothing	_____	14 ghost	_____
15 grow	_____	15 boats	_____	15 drown	_____	15 groan	_____
16 frog	_____	16 blow	_____	16 plate	_____	16 servants	_____
17 struck	_____	17 great	_____	17 scent	_____	17 pitcher	_____
18 birthday	_____	18 there's	_____	18 disappointed	_____	18 perched	_____
19 peanut	_____	19 mouth	_____	19 posture	_____	19 weight	_____
20 don't	_____	20 mail	_____	20 pale	_____	20 knowledge	_____
	_____ %		_____ %		_____ %		_____ %

Teacher note: If the student missed five words in any column—stop Part 1. Begin Graded Paragraphs, Part 2, (Form D), at highest level in which all 20 words were recognized. To save time, if the first ten words were correct, go on to the next list. If one of the first ten words was missed, continue the entire list.

Form C Part 1/Graded Word Lists

5		**6**		**7**		**8**	
1 whether	_____	1 moisture	_____	1 numberless	_____	1 pulverized	_____
2 notched	_____	2 dorsal	_____	2 derby	_____	2 custody	_____
3 sandals	_____	3 contrary	_____	3 omen	_____	3 delusion	_____
4 pronged	_____	4 sausage	_____	4 rayon	_____	4 barbarian	_____
5 sprinkle	_____	5 notions	_____	5 accumulate	_____	5 privacy	_____
6 shrill	_____	6 pounce	_____	6 dense	_____	6 embankment	_____
7 length	_____	7 envelope	_____	7 potential	_____	7 designate	_____
8 contest	_____	8 request	_____	8 terrain	_____	8 notorious	_____
9 muscle	_____	9 wreath	_____	9 vivid	_____	9 arrogant	_____
10 chant	_____	10 knights	_____	10 segment	_____	10 quote	_____
11 excused	_____	11 irregular	_____	11 amber	_____	11 variation	_____
12 vinegar	_____	12 torrent	_____	12 humidity	_____	12 pneumonia	_____
13 shuffled	_____	13 salad	_____	13 monarch	_____	13 embassy	_____
14 pierce	_____	14 applause	_____	14 publication	_____	14 yacht	_____
15 bore	_____	15 hustling	_____	15 meteorite	_____	15 authentic	_____
16 delicious	_____	16 tenor	_____	16 ridicule	_____	16 brigade	_____
17 orchard	_____	17 hearth	_____	17 domestic	_____	17 browse	_____
18 territory	_____	18 surf	_____	18 focus	_____	18 recruit	_____
19 pouches	_____	19 condition	_____	19 irregular	_____	19 motive	_____
20 plateau	_____	20 official	_____	20 algebra	_____	20 belligerent	_____
	_____ %		_____ %		_____ %		_____ %

Background Knowledge Assessment. What can you tell me about grasshoppers?[18]

adequate ☐   inadequate ☐

Grasshoppers

Grasshoppers come from eggs.

They have four long wings and six legs.

Some grasshoppers live on the ground, others live in

trees.

All grasshoppers can jump and fly.

They fly high in the air.

They jump, fly, and play.

Most grasshoppers are green, black, or brown.

Comprehension Check

(F)   1. _____ How many legs do grasshoppers have?
(Six)

(F)   2. _____ Where do grasshoppers come from?
(Eggs)

(F)   3. _____ Not all grasshoppers are the same color.
Name two colors for them.
(Green, black, or brown)

(F)   4. _____ Name two things that grasshoppers do.
(Fly, jump, play, etc.)

(I)   5. _____ Where are some places that grasshoppers
can hide?
(Grass, weeds or trees difficult to reach)

Scoring Guide   First

SIG WR Errors		COMP Errors	
IND	0	IND	0–1
INST	2	INST	1½–2
FRUST	5	FRUST	2½+

18. See page 5 for a discussion of Background Knowledge Assessment.

Form C Part 2 / *Level 2* (78 words)

Background Knowledge Assessment.   Much has been told about astronauts and the John F. Kennedy Space Center. Tell me things you remember.   adequate ☐   inadequate ☐

The John F. Kennedy Space Center

A ball of fire is seen in the sky. The sky turns red

and orange.

Another rocket has been tested!

Most rocket tests are made in Florida.

The first test was made in 1958.

In 1969 men were sent to the moon.

People near the space center see

rockets going off all the time.

Almost every day is like the Fourth of July. We do

not shoot them just for fun.

We hope to learn things about space.

Comprehension Check

(F)   1. _____ Why do we send rockets into space?
(Learn things about space)

(F)   2. _____ The story said that the sky turns color when rockets are tested, name one.
(Red or orange)

(F)   3. _____ How often do people see the rockets going off?
(All of the time)

(F)   4. _____ The story said that most tests were made in what state?
(Florida)

(I)   5. _____ Rocket testing is like the Fourth of July, why?
(People shoot firecrackers and sky rockets on the 4th)

Scoring Guide   Second

SIG WR Errors		COMP Errors	
IND	1	IND	0–1
INST	3–4	INST	1½–2
FRUST	6	FRUST	2½+

Background Knowledge Assessment. Have you visited a National Park? (If yes, tell about it.) (If no, can you guess what these parks are like?)   adequate ☐   inadequate ☐

Yellowstone National Park

Each year more than two million people visit Yellowstone National Park.

It is the largest of our national parks.

The park is more than 8,000 feet above sea level.

It has many natural hot water fountains called geysers. "Old Faithful" is the best-known of the geysers. It is not the largest, but is famous because it is so regular in its activity. "Old Faithful" shoots water and steam over 120 feet in the air. It does this about every 73 minutes, summer and winter. It has been doing this since early times. You can see why so many people visit this great park.

Comprehension Check

(F) 1. _____ How many people visit Yellowstone National Park each year?
(Over two million)

(F) 2. _____ What is the name of one of the park's famous geysers?
(Old Faithful)

(F) 3. _____ What is a geyser?
(Deep hole in ground, water and steam shoot up from it)

(F) 4. _____ Water and steam shoots out of Old Faithful (geyser in this story) how often?
(About every 73 min.)

(I) 5. _____ Why is "Old Faithful's" name a good one?
(It is regular in its activity, summer and winter)

Scoring Guide Third

SIG WR Errors		COMP Errors	
IND	2	IND	0–1
INST	5	INST	1½–2
FRUST	10	FRUST	2½+

Background Knowledge Assessment. Most everyone has played baseball or softball. Tell me what you know about this popular game. adequate ☐ inadequate ☐

A Great American Sport

The history of baseball shows that the game has changed a great deal since it was first played. In 1839, Abner Doubleday set up the rules for playing a baseball game.

Later on, uniforms appeared. The players wore long pants, a fancy white shirt, and a straw hat. The umpire wore a long coat, a tall silk hat, and carried a cane. Rakes, ax handles, and tree branches were used as bats.

The first World Series was played in 1903. Baseball fans wanted to see the top teams from the two major leagues play. The winners would be the champions of the baseball world.

Comprehension Check

(F) 1. ____ What year were the rules set up for baseball?
(1839)

(F) 2. ____ Several things were used as baseball bats, name two.
(Rakes or ax handles, tree branches)

(V) 3. ____ What does "fan" mean in this story?
(A person interested in a sport or movie star.)

(F) 4. ____ What were the first player uniforms like?
(Long pants, fancy shirts, straw hat)

(I) 5. ____ Why does professional baseball have a World Series?
(So two top teams can play or two teams play for the championship)

Scoring Guide   Fourth

SIG WR Errors		COMP Errors	
IND	2	IND	0–1
INST	5	INST	1½–2
FRUST	10+	FRUST	2½+

Background Knowledge Assessment. Why is Driver Education an important class or program?

adequate ☐   inadequate ☐

Driver Education

Even our parents may have some bad driving habits. This is why young drivers should take lessons from trained teachers.

A recent story makes this point. A young driver had learned from an older one. While driving, a young driver felt his two right wheels go off the road. He yanked the car quickly back onto the road. As a result, the car turned over. A passenger in the car was killed. A trained teacher would have taught the driver not to slam on the brakes. And not to turn back onto the road too quickly.

One of the best ways to decrease traffic accidents is to have more driver education.

Comprehension Check

(F) 1. _____ What happened when the young driver yanked the car back onto the road?
(Car turned over)

(F) 2. _____ When the car turned over what happened to a passenger?
(Person was killed)

(F) 3. _____ What does "decrease" mean?
(Make smaller, less)

(I) 4. _____ Why is it better to take driving lessons from a trained teacher than an older driver?
(A trained teacher knows more about driver training)

(I) 5. _____ What caused the car to turn over?
(Two right wheels were caught or jammed on the pavement or road)

Scoring Guide Fifth

SIG WR Errors		COMP Errors	
IND	2	IND	0–1
INST	6	INST	1½–2
FRUST	11	FRUST	2½+

Form C Part 2 / *Level 6* (116 words)

Background Knowledge Assessment. If I use words such as white-tailed deer, meadows, woods and hunting what do you think about?   adequate ☐   inadequate ☐

Sentinels in the Forest

Many wild creatures that travel with their own kind know by instinct how to protect the group. One of them acts as a sentinel.

Hidden by the branches of a low-hanging tree, I once watched two white-tailed deer feeding in a meadow. At first, my interest was held by their beauty. But soon I noticed something which was quite unusual; they were taking turns at feeding.

One deer was calmly cropping grass, unafraid and at ease. The other, a sentinel, stood guard against enemies. The guard deer watched every movement and used its sensitive nostrils to "feel" the air. Not for a moment, during the half hour I spied upon them, did they stop their teamwork.

Comprehension Check

(F) 1. ____ Where was the author as he watched the deer?
(Hidden by branches of a low-hanging tree)

(V) 2. ____ What is a "sentinel"?
(One who stands guard)

(I) 3. ____ Why was the deer that was eating calm and unafraid?
(Knew the other deer or sentinel was standing guard)

(V) 4. ____ What do "used its sensitive nostrils to 'feel' the air" mean?
(Had a good sense of smell and was smelling the air for a scent of an enemy)

(V) 5. ____ What does "cropping grass" mean in the story?
(Eating the grass)

Scoring Guide Sixth

SIG WR Errors		COMP Errors	
IND	2	IND	0–1
INST	6	INST	1½–2
FRUST	11	FRUST	2½+

Background Knowledge Assessment. What airport can you name? Tell me about this airport or any others.

adequate ☐   inadequate ☐

Modern Airports

In the earliest days of aviation, there was no need for airports. The light wood-and-cloth airplanes could take off and land in any level, open field.

In contrast to these simple airfields, the modern airport is almost a city in itself. There are many buildings and services for the convenience and comfort of the passengers.

Waiting rooms, restaurants, barbershops, post offices, banks, souvenir shops, florists, and even bowling alleys are likely to be located in the airport.

But the heart of the airport is still the area where the planes take off and land—the runways. Jet planes require very long runways—sometimes as much as two miles in length. Runways are paved with concrete to withstand the impact of planes weighing over 375 tons hitting the ground at speeds between 110 and 140 miles per hour. Taxiways link the runways with each other and with terminal buildings.

Comprehension Check

(F) 1. ＿＿ Why were airports unnecessary in the early days of aviation?
(Planes were light, slow, short take off, etc.)

(F) 2. ＿＿ Name three customer services found at modern airports.
(Restaurants, barbershop, post office, bank, etc.)

(F) 3. ＿＿ Approximately how heavy are the large jets?
(They weigh over 375 tons)

(I) 4. ＿＿ Why do jets require long runways?
(Planes are heavy and fast, long stop and take off, etc.)

(V) 5. ＿＿ What does "impact" mean?
(Violent contact, collision, etc.)

Scoring Guide   Seventh

SIG WR Errors		COMP Errors	
IND	3	IND	0–1
INST	7–8	INST	1½–2
FRUST	15	FRUST	2½+

Background Knowledge Assessment. The author seems to have strong opinions about American sport cars. Before you read the story can you guess what they are?   adequate ☐   inadequate ☐

Sports Cars

To most laymen, a sports car is simply a vehicle with a flashy, streamlined body decorated with plenty of chrome. Such a vehicle, however, might easily be everything that an actual sports car should not be. It is the engineering features that the untrained eye does not observe which distinguish the true sports car from the bloated, over-chromed and highly colored dream cars that cruise along the American freeways on weekend afternoons.

The meticulously engineered features of a genuine sports car are those observed on the road rather than those idolized in the parking lots of country clubs. That which ordinarily is referred to as an American sports car would not be permitted to enter a European road race, because it would be too unsafe both for its own operator and for the other participants in a race. For another thing, it would be ridiculously outclassed for acceleration and road-ability under conditions of such competitive driving.

Comprehension Check

(V)   1. _____ What does the author mean by the word "laymen"?
(A person untrained in a specific field or area)

(F)   2. _____ What do most Americans think sports cars are?
(Flashy, decorated body, etc.)

(F)   3. _____ The American sports car, usually found on our highways, would not be permitted in European road races. Why not?
(Unsafe, not well engineered, etc.)

(V)   4. _____ What does "meticulously" mean?
(Extremely careful about details)

(I)   5. _____ What is the author's opinion of American sports cars?
(They are incorrect, misguided, etc.)

Scoring Guide   Eighth

SIG WR Errors		COMP Errors	
IND	3	IND	0–1
INST	7–8	INST	1½–2
FRUST	15	FRUST	2½+

FORM D

Part 1 Graded Word Lists

Designed for High School Students and Adults

Form D

1 then	1 mouth
2 place	2 boats
3 garbage	3 together
4 grow	4 chipmunk
5 birthday	5 wheels
6 don't	6 clang
7 night	7 slide
8 men	8 deer
9 flowers	9 both
10 fire	10 room
11 her	11 horn
12 eight	12 beautiful
13 stopping	13 sorry
14 let's	14 climb
15 frog	15 head
16 trucks	16 corn
17 cannot	17 strong
18 feet	18 blows
19 garden	19 that's
20 drop	20 own

Form D

1 soup	1 barrel
2 remember	2 nephew
3 enemy	3 experience
4 inventor	4 trousers
5 enough	5 iron
6 unusual	6 ghost
7 disappointed	7 groan
8 posture	8 weight
9 hour	9 pedal
10 direction	10 machine
11 escape	11 force
12 matter	12 weather
13 unhappy	13 island
14 discover	14 predict
15 turkeys	15 knowledge
16 either	16 spoon
17 pencil	17 dozen
18 nail	18 exercise
19 senseless	19 bound
20 clothes	20 rooster

Form D

1 plateau

2 bore

3 vinegar

4 muscle

5 sandals

6 contest

7 freedom

8 examined

9 scarf

10 oars

11 octave

12 salmon

13 briskly

14 delicious

15 pacing

16 considerable

17 musical

18 scientist

19 amount

20 hymn

1 moisture

2 dorsal

3 envelope

4 request

5 knights

6 applause

7 culprit

8 demon

9 wreath

10 torrent

11 liberty

12 blond

13 marsh

14 customer

15 hearth

16 pounce

17 instinct

18 billows

19 sensitive

20 nostrils

Form D

1 plasma	1 coagulate
2 alternative	2 surgical
3 barometer	3 optimistic
4 joyous	4 disposition
5 dialects	5 metaphor
6 mystical	6 controversy
7 taco	7 exchange
8 exploited	8 imperative
9 thermostat	9 demeanor
10 vigorously	10 futility
11 attainment	11 absolutely
12 logical	12 foggy
13 geologist	13 ardently
14 resource	14 perch
15 fundamental	15 immortal
16 compliment	16 pliers
17 carbonation	17 obsolete
18 senators	18 speculate
19 condense	19 admiral
20 biscuits	20 keel

FORM D

Part 2 Graded Paragraphs

Designed for High School Students and Adults

The Car Wash

Diane's car needed cleaning. She went to the car wash. The man asked what she wanted. "Just a wash," said Diane. The man asked, "How about gas?"

"No, just a wash," she said.

Then the man asked about hot wax. "No, just a wash," she said.

"Wow! People are always selling something," said Diane.

Lizards Are Smart

Lizards use many ways to protect themselves. Some lizards can blow up to three times their size. Others can keep running even if their tail is pulled off. All they do is just grow a new tail. There are even lizards that can swim.

Most lizards move in funny ways. They can walk or run upside-down. They can run on their two back legs. Lizards are quick and can leap from place to place.

If you don't think that lizards are smart, try to catch one.

Hang Gliding

Hang gliding? Some people think that this new sport is called hand gliding. "Hang," "hand"—it doesn't take much to cause confusion.

Hang gliding got its start in the early 1970s. California is likely to have the most hang glider pilots. Hang gliders are made by attaching a triangular sail to a frame. The glider is about 32 feet wide. The pilot takes off by holding the glider and running down the windward side of a cliff. When airborne, the pilot steers the glider with a control bar.

Hang glider pilots must be well trained. It is a good sport for both men and women.

Forest Fire Fighters

Fighting forest fires is hard work. Forest fires are difficult to stop when water is not available. Fire fighters have to use other ways to stop fires. They dig fire lines. This is a long cleared strip in front of the fire. The fire line keeps the flames from spreading. The fire line also holds the fire in a small area. Fire fighters work back from this line to put out the fire. Sometimes smoke jumpers are used to fight fires. They parachute into out-of-the-way places to put out fires. A new way to stop forest fires is called slurry bombing. Airplanes drop liquid in front of the fire to slow it down. With a lot of skill and a little luck, fire fighters can save our forests.

College Football

College football began when Princeton played Rutgers in 1869. Soon other colleges began playing football. Different rules were added each year. Some schools added passing. Others added scoring. Even the size of the field was different. Finally, in 1905 a national committee was formed. This committee made rules for all schools to follow.

In the early days football was a simple game. One team just ran the ball around or over the other. Today football is complex. It takes months for players to learn the plays. Colleges are grouped into conferences. For example, the winner of the PAC-10 and BIG 10 play each other in the Rose Bowl Game. Football is the most popular college sport. We all know when it's fall because football is everywhere.

Hey Kid, This Is the U.S. Open

It was 1979 when the big tennis event happened. Tracy Austin, age 16, won the U.S. Tennis Open. When Tracy beat Chris Evert, she became the youngest player to win the Open. No player, male or female, had ever won the Open at this young age.

Few people actually thought Tracy had a chance to win. Even her coach did not believe she could win. In fact, he vowed to quit smoking if she won. Tracy reminded him about the no smoking vow when the match was over.

Tracy Austin beat Evert by being steady and consistent. Evert was rocked by critical mistakes throughout the match. When the match was over Tracy shouted, "I can't believe it! I really did win!"

Burro Lift

What do you do with 400 burros who are over-grazing in Arizona's Grand Canyon? This was a difficult problem for the U.S. Park Service. As one person put it, "Those burros are in a hole a mile deep."

After thinking about many things, the U.S. Park Service decided to shoot the burros. A group called Fund for Animals opposed the Park Service plan. With the Park Service's OK, the group began removing the burros by helicopter. Rounding up burros in a hot canyon was a hard job. Another problem was flying them out of the canyon. Then came the greatest job of all, finding a new home for the burros.

The Fund for Animals group and another group, called the National Organization for Wild American Horses, put the burros up for adoption.

The most important thing about the burro lift was that when people decide to work together they can overcome problems.

The White Shark

Scientists tell us that there are about 350 kinds of sharks. Of this total, approximately ten percent are known to be man-eating. The most dangerous of the man-eating sharks is the white shark. This killer can grow up to 40 feet long and devour a six-foot man whole.

According to scientists, white sharks and other man-eaters rely on their nose to locate food. Scientists conducted two types of experiments to prove this. They starved a shark, then dropped a small amount of fish juice into the water. The shark immediately became excited. Scientists plugged up the nostrils of a man-eating shark. In this situation, the shark could not tell the difference between a bag of food and a bag of marbles.

No one knows why or when sharks will attack. The best advice for man is to leave sharks alone, especially white sharks.

F O R M   D

Inventory Record for Teachers

Designed for High School Students and Adults

Form D may be used in any of the following ways.
1. As a set of *silent paragraphs* for students who
   might reject oral reading
2. As a set of *silent paragraphs* used with Form C
3. As a set of *paragraphs* for assessing the
   student's listening capacity level. (see p. 8)

Form D Inventory Record _____

Summary Sheet

Student's Name _____ Grade _____ Age (Chronological) _____

Date _____ School _____ Administered by _____

yrs. mos.

Part 1 Word Lists			Part 2 Graded Paragraphs		
Grade Level	Percent of Words Correct	Word Recognition Errors			
			SIG WR	Comp	L.C.

Part 1 — Word Lists

Grade Level	Percent of Words Correct	Word Recognition Errors
1	_____	Consonants
		____ consonants
		____ blends
		____ digraphs
		____ endings
		____ compounds
		____ contractions
2	_____	Vowels
		____ long
		____ short
		____ long/short oo
		____ vowel + r
		____ diphthong
		____ vowel comb.
		____ a + 1 or w
3	_____	Syllable
		____ visual patterns
		____ prefix
4	_____	____ suffix
5	_____	Word Recognition
6	_____	reinforcement and
7	_____	Vocabulary
8	_____	development

Part 2 — Graded Paragraphs

	SIG WR	Comp	L.C.
PP			
P			
1			
2			
3			
4			
5			
6			
7			
8			

Estimated Levels

	Grade
Independent	_____
Instructional	_____ (range)
Frustration	_____
Listening Capacity	_____

Comp Errors

_____ Factual (F)

_____ Inference (I)

_____ Vocabulary (V)

_____ "Word Caller"
(A student who reads without associating meaning)

_____ Poor Memory

Summary of Specific Needs:

1		2		3		4	
1 then	————	1 mouth	————	1 soup	————	1 barrel	————
2 place	————	2 boats	————	2 remember	————	2 nephew	————
3 garbage	————	3 together	————	3 enemy	————	3 experience	————
4 grow	————	4 chipmunk	————	4 inventor	————	4 trousers	————
5 birthday	————	5 wheels	————	5 enough	————	5 iron	————
6 don't	————	6 clang	————	6 unusual	————	6 ghost	————
7 night	————	7 slide	————	7 disappointed	————	7 groan	————
8 men	————	8 deer	————	8 posture	————	8 weight	————
9 flowers	————	9 both	————	9 hour	————	9 pedal	————
10 fire	————	10 room	————	10 direction	————	10 machine	————
11 her	————	11 horn	————	11 escape	————	11 force	————
12 eight	————	12 beautiful	————	12 matter	————	12 weather	————
13 stopping	————	13 sorry	————	13 unhappy	————	13 island	————
14 let's	————	14 climb	————	14 discover	————	14 predict	————
15 frog	————	15 head	————	15 turkeys	————	15 knowledge	————
16 trucks	————	16 corn	————	16 either	————	16 spoon	————
17 cannot	————	17 strong	————	17 pencil	————	17 dozen	————
18 feet	————	18 blows	————	18 nail	————	18 exercise	————
19 garden	————	19 that's	————	19 senseless	————	19 bound	————
20 drop	————	20 own	————	20 clothes	————	20 rooster	————
———— %		———— %		———— %		———— %	

Teacher note: If the child misses five words in any column, stop Part 1. Begin Graded Paragraphs, Part 2 (Form A), at the highest level in which the child recognized all 20 words. To save time, if the first ten words were correct, go on to the next list. If one of the words was missed, continue the entire list.

Form D Part 1/Graded Word Lists

5		6		7		8	
1 plateau	————	1 moisture	————	1 plasma	————	1 coagulate	————
2 bore	————	2 dorsal	————	2 alternative	————	2 surgical	————
3 vinegar	————	3 envelope	————	3 barometer	————	3 optimistic	————
4 muscle	————	4 request	————	4 joyous	————	4 disposition	————
5 sandals	————	5 knights	————	5 dialects	————	5 metaphor	————
6 contest	————	6 applause	————	6 mystical	————	6 controversy	————
7 freedom	————	7 culprit	————	7 taco	————	7 exchange	————
8 examined	————	8 demon	————	8 exploited	————	8 imperative	————
9 scarf	————	9 wreath	————	9 thermostat	————	9 demeanor	————
10 oars	————	10 torrent	————	10 vigorously	————	10 futility	————
11 octave	————	11 liberty	————	11 attainment	————	11 absolutely	————
12 salmon	————	12 blond	————	12 logical	————	12 foggy	————
13 briskly	————	13 marsh	————	13 geologist	————	13 ardently	————
14 delicious	————	14 customer	————	14 resource	————	14 perch	————
15 pacing	————	15 hearth	————	15 fundamental	————	15 immortal	————
16 considerable	————	16 pounce	————	16 compliment	————	16 pliers	————
17 musical	————	17 instinct	————	17 carbonation	————	17 obsolete	————
18 scientist	————	18 billows	————	18 senators	————	18 speculate	————
19 amount	————	19 sensitive	————	19 condense	————	19 admiral	————
20 hymn	————	20 nostrils	————	20 biscuits	————	20 keel	————
———— %		———— %		———— %		———— %	

Background Knowledge Assessment. What things do you have to do when you wash a car?[19]

adequate ☐   inadequate ☐

The Car Wash

Diane's car needed cleaning. She went to the car wash. The man asked what she wanted. "Just a wash," said Diane. The man asked, "How about gas?"

"No, just a wash," she said.

Then the man asked about hot wax. "No, just a wash," she said.

"Wow! People are always selling something," said Diane.

Comprehension Check

(F) 1. _____ Who went to the car wash?
(Diane or a girl)

(I) 2. _____ About how old was this person (Diane)? If you are not sure, guess.
(At least sixteen or over sixteen years of age)

(F) 3. _____ What two things did the man want to sell?
(Gas and hot wax, car wash)

(V) 4. _____ What does "always selling something" mean?
(Trying to sell extra items, selling more)

(I) 5. _____ How did the person (Diane) feel about all the extra service offered?
(Surprised, didn't like it)

Scoring Guide   First

SIG WR Errors		COMP Errors	
IND	0	IND	0–1
INST	2	INST	1½–2
FRUST	4+	FRUST	2½+

19. See page 5 for a discussion of Background Knowledge Assessment.

Form D Part 2/ *Level 2* (87 words)

Background Knowledge Assessment. Most zoos have a variety of lizards. You probably know things about lizards. Tell me about them.

adequate☐   inadequate☐

Lizards Are Smart

Lizards use many ways to protect themselves. Some lizards can blow up to three times their size. Others can keep running even if their tail is pulled off. All they do is just grow a new tail. There are even lizards that can swim.

Most lizards move in funny ways. They can walk or run upside-down. They can run on their two back legs. Lizards are quick and can leap from place to place.

If you don't think that lizards are smart, try to catch one.

Comprehension Check

(F) 1. ____ Give two ways in which lizards protect themselves.
(Blow up or increase size, hide, move in funny ways, leap, etc.)

(V) 2. ____ Give a word that means about the same as "protect."
(Defend, guard, preserve)

(F) 3. ____ What happens to a lizard if its tail is pulled off?
(Nothing, grows another)

(F) 4. ____ Why is it hard to catch a lizard?
(They're smart, quick, and/or can leap)

(I) 5. ____ How does the author feel about lizards?
(Likes them, thinks they are smart)

Scoring Guide Second

SIG WR Errors		COMP Errors	
IND	1	IND	0–1
INST	4	INST	1½–2
FRUST	8+	FRUST	2½+

Background Knowledge Assessment. Hang (not hand) gliding is a new sport. Hang gliders use wind currents when gliding. What do you know about this new sport?   adequate ☐   inadequate ☐

Hang Gliding

Hang gliding? Some people think that this new sport is called hand gliding. "Hang," "hand" it doesn't take much to cause confusion.

Hang gliding got its start in the early 1970s. California is likely to have the most hang glider pilots. Hang gliders are made by attaching a triangular sail to a frame. The glider is about 32 feet wide. The pilot takes off by holding the glider and running down the windward side of a cliff. When airborne, the pilot steers the glider with a control bar.

Hang glider pilots must be well trained. It is a good sport for both men and women.

Comprehension Check

(F)   1. _____ What state is likely to have the most hang glider pilots?
(California)

(F)   2. _____ About how wide is a hang glider?
(Thirty-two feet)

(V)   3. _____ Describe a "triangular" sail.
(Three sides)

(F)   4. _____ How does a pilot change the direction of the glider?
(With a control bar)

(I)   5. _____ Why do hang glider pilots need to be well trained?
(Misjudge air, crash, person can get killed)

Scoring Guide   Third

SIG WR Errors		COMP Errors	
IND	2	IND	0–1
INST	5–6	INST	1½–2
FRUST	11+	FRUST	2½+

Form D Part 2 / *Level 4* (131 words)

Background Knowledge Assessment. Forest fires are dangerous. Once a fire is started can you tell some ways to put the fire out?   adequate ☐   inadequate ☐

Forest Fire Fighters

Fighting forest fires is hard work. Forest fires are difficult to stop when water is not available. Fire fighters have to use other ways to stop fires. They dig fire lines. This is a long cleared strip in front of the fire. The fire line keeps the flames from spreading. The fire line also holds the fire in a small area. Fire fighters work back from this line to put out the fire. Sometimes smoke jumpers are used to fight fires. They parachute into out-of-the-way places to put out fires. A new way to stop forest fires is called slurry bombing. Airplanes drop liquid in front of the fire to slow it down. With a lot of skill and a little luck, fire fighters can save our forests.

Comprehension Check

(F) 1. _____ Why are forest fires difficult to stop?
(Lack of water to put out fires, fires in out-of-way places)

(F) 2. _____ What are fire lines?
(Long cleared strips which keep fires from spreading)

(I) 3. _____ If there were strong winds directly from the west, where would you put the fire line?
(On the east, facing the wind and fire)

(V) 4. _____ What is slurry?
(A liquid used to slow down or smother fires)

(F) 5. _____ What do smoke jumpers do?
(Jump-parachute to out-of-the-way fires, put out fires)

Scoring Guide Fourth

SIG WR Errors		COMP Errors	
IND	2	IND	0–1
INST	6	INST	1½–2
FRUST	12+	FRUST	2½+

Background Knowledge Assessment. When I use words such as pass, tackle, run, cheerleaders, and quarterback you are probably thinking of football. Tell me about football.　　adequate ☐　　inadequate ☐

College Football

College football began when Princeton played Rutgers in 1869. Soon other colleges began playing football. Different rules were added each year. Some schools added passing. Others added scoring. Even the size of the field was different. Finally, in 1905 a national committee was formed. This committee made rules for all schools to follow.

In the early days football was a simple game. One team just ran the ball around or over the other. Today football is complex. It takes months for players to learn the plays. Colleges are grouped into conferences. For example, the winner of the PAC-10 and BIG 10 play each other in the Rose Bowl Game. Football is the most popular college sport. We all know when it's fall because football is everywhere.

Comprehension Check

(F)　1. ____ Can you name one of the first colleges to play football?
(Princeton or Rutgers)

(F)　2. ____ Why was a national athletic committee formed in 1905?
(To make rules or standardize the game of football)

(F)　3. ____ What was said that makes you think that football was simple in the early days?
(One team just ran around or over)

(I)　4. ____ How did they get the ball down the field before passing was allowed?
(Ran the ball)

(V)　5. ____ What is meant by "colleges are grouped into conferences"?
(A number of teams agree to work together or play each other)

Scoring Guide　Fifth

SIG WR Errors		COMP Errors	
IND	2	IND	0–1
INST	6	INST	1½–2
FRUST	12+	FRUST	2½+

Background Knowledge Assessment. Tennis is another popular sport. Have you ever played tennis? Tell me about this sport.   adequate ☐   inadequate ☐

Hey Kid, This Is the U.S. Open

It was 1979 when the big tennis event happened. Tracy Austin, age 16, won the U.S. Tennis Open. When Tracy beat Chris Evert, she became the youngest player to win the Open. No player, male or female, had ever won the Open at this young age.

Few people actually thought Tracy had a chance to win. Even her coach did not believe she could win. In fact, he vowed to quit smoking if she won. Tracy reminded him about the "no smoking" vow when the match was over.

Tracy Austin beat Evert by being steady and consistent. Evert was rocked by critical mistakes throughout the match. When the match was over Tracy shouted, "I can't believe it! I really did win!"

Comprehension Check

(F)   1. _____ This story was about what young tennis player?
(Tracy Austin)

(F)   2. _____ How old was she when she won the U.S. Open?
(Sixteen)

(V)   3. _____ What does "vowed" mean?
(Agreed to do something, promised)

(I)   4. _____ Why did the coach probably have another feeling besides happiness after the win?
(He had to quit smoking)

(F)   5. _____ Why did Tracy beat Chris Evert?
(She was better, was consistent, didn't make as many mistakes)

Scoring Guide   Sixth

SIG WR Errors		COMP Errors	
IND	2	IND	0–1
INST	6	INST	1½–2
FRUST	12+	FRUST	2½+

Background Knowledge Assessment. Imagine getting burros out of Arizona's Grand Canyon. What problems would a group have if they tried to get burros out of the steep walled Grand Canyon?

adequate ☐   inadequate ☐

Burro Lift

What do you do with 400 burros who are over-grazing in Arizona's Grand Canyon? This was a difficult problem for the U.S. Park Service. As one person put it, "Those burros are in a hole a mile deep."

After thinking about many things, the U.S. Park Service decided to shoot the burros. A group called Fund for Animals opposed the Park Service plan. With the Park Service's OK, the group began removing the burros by helicopter. Rounding up burros in a hot canyon was a hard job. Another problem was flying them out of the canyon. Then came the greatest job of all, finding a new home for the burros.

The Fund for Animals group and another group, called the National Organization for Wild American Horses, put the burros up for adoption.

The most important thing about the burro lift was that when people decide to work together they can overcome problems.

Comprehension Check

(V) 1. _____ What is meant by over-grazing?
(Too much grass or vegetation is eaten, not enough food for other animals)

(I) 2. _____ Why not just walk the burros out of the Grand Canyon?
(Sides of Canyon too steep or it says a hole a mile deep)

(F) 3. _____ How did the U.S. Park Service plan to remove the burros?
(Shoot them)

(F) 4. _____ How did the Fund for Animals remove the burros?
(Flew them out by helicopter)

(V) 5. _____ Give me a word that means to work together or to work for a common purpose.
(Cooperate, association, etc.)

Scoring Guide   Seventh

SIG WR Errors		COMP Errors	
IND	3	IND	0–1
INST	7	INST	1½–2
FRUST	14+	FRUST	2½+

Background Knowledge Assessment. Did you see the movie Jaws? (If, yes, tell about it.) (If no, have you seen a movie about sharks?)   adequate ☐   inadequate ☐

The White Shark

Scientists tell us that there are about 350 kinds of sharks. Of this total, approximately ten percent are known to be man-eating. The most dangerous of the man-eating sharks is the white shark. This killer can grow up to 40 feet long and devour a six-foot man whole.

According to scientists, white sharks and other man-eaters rely on their nose to locate food. Scientists conducted two types of experiments to prove this. They starved a shark, then dropped a small amount of fish juice into the water. The shark immediately became excited. Scientists plugged up the nostrils of a man-eating shark. In this situation, the shark could not tell the difference between a bag of food and a bag of marbles.

No one knows why or when sharks will attack. The best advice for man is to leave sharks alone, especially white sharks.

Comprehension Check

(F) 1. ____ About what percent of sharks are man-eating?
(10 percent)

(F) 2. ____ What do white sharks use to locate food?
(Their nose or smell)

(V) 3. ____ What does "experiment" mean?
(To prove, demonstrate, or find out something)

(F) 4. ____ In one experiment a man-eating shark could not tell the difference between food and marbles, why?
(Nostrils or nose plugged, couldn't smell anything)

(F) 5. ____ Why is it dangerous to bleed in water where sharks are?
(Can smell it)

Scoring Guide   Eighth

SIG WR Errors		COMP Errors	
IND	3	IND	0–1
INST	7	INST	1½–2
FRUST	14+	FRUST	2½+

Graded Spelling Survey

Graded Spelling Survey Words

1. Pronounce the word.
2. Use the word in a sentence.
3. Pronounce the word again.
4. Ask the student to spell the word.

1	2	3
1 some	1 table	1 news
2 go	2 you	2 things
3 he	3 bed	3 six
4 mother	4 must	4 teacher
5 was	5 have	5 roof
6 in	6 water	6 farmer
7 do	7 many	7 walked
8 it	8 five	8 ready
9 can	9 other	9 part
10 with	10 much	10 carry

4	5	6
1 choose	1 delay	1 central
2 witch	2 owner	2 prevent
3 fit	3 laid	3 profit
4 burned	4 seventeen	4 serving
5 forest	5 parties	5 directly
6 raise	6 study	6 material
7 learn	7 airplane	7 wherever
8 given	8 having	8 adventure
9 everyone	9 strike	9 canvas
10 turkey	10 bucket	10 pleased